TRUE GENIUS

TRUE GENIUS

1001 QUOTES THAT WILL CHANGE YOUR LIFE

ELIZABETH VENSTRA

SKYHORSE PUBLISHING

Skyhorse Publishing books may be purchased in bulk at special discounts for sales promotion, corporate gifts, fund raising, or educational purposes. Special editions can also be created to specifications. For details, contact the Special Sales Department, Skyhorse Publishing, 555 Eighth Avenue, Suite 903, New York, NY 10018 or info@skyhorsepublishing.com.

www.skyhorsepublishing.com

10 9 8 7 6 5 4 3 2 1

Library of Congress Cataloging-in-Publication Data

True genius : 1001 quotes that will change your life / [edited by] Elizabeth Venstra.
    p. cm.
 ISBN 978-1-60239-334-9 (alk. paper)
 1. Quotations, English. I. Venstra, Elizabeth.
 PN6081.T78 2008
 808.88'2--dc22

                        2008019308

Printed in China

CONTENTS

Introduction vii

Chapter 1: Life in the Universe 1

Chapter 2: Identity and the Self 43

Chapter 3: Character and Personal Action 89

Chapter 4: Truth 127

Chapter 5: Guiding Emotions 167

Chapter 6: Dreams, Desires, and Personal Quests 203

Chapter 7: Success and Greatness 243

Chapter 8: Time 289

Chapter 9: Relationships 333

Chapter 10: The Self in the World 377

Index 421

Introduction

Of course you know at the outset that the title of this book exaggerates. It implies that each of the 1,001 quotes in this book will, of themselves, change the life of the individual reader, whoever you are. Such a collection is an obvious impossibility. Even if I knew what you in particular needed to hear to change your life, and even supposing I were lucky enough to find a thousand quotes that all conveyed personalized messages to you with life-changing urgency, still some of those quotes would leave your next-door neighbor absolutely unmoved. As Emerson said: "Take the book, my friend, and read your eyes out, you will never find there what I find." So while I cannot possibly compile a thousand quotes that will really change your life, my hope is simply that somewhere in this book, you may find at least a few quotes that speak to you where you are right now.

And perhaps you will want to speak back to some of them. I hope that you won't agree with all of the quotes in this book; I don't. To do so would be contradictory, since some of the ideas here conflict with others; in fact, I've deliberately juxtaposed some of these quotes to highlight the contrasts between them. But just because two quotes contradict each other, does that necessarily mean that you can't agree with both of them? As Thomas Mann put it, "A great truth is a truth whose opposite is also a great truth." And please don't assume that the authors I play off against each other would necessarily disagree with each other if we could bring them together to talk the matter over (although some almost certainly would). Often they are simply talking about different faces of the same stone. At other times they are talking about different things altogether, even when they use the same words. Words are slippery things, and all readers are hereby advised to be on their guard.

The quotations in this book come from all sorts of people. Many of them are famous; others were well-known once, but may be forgotten by most people now; a few are just ordinary folks. I believe that a good number of them are or were truly geniuses of one kind or another—not only in the sense of one with great abilities and achievements, but perhaps also in an older sense of the word. The oldest meaning given for "genius" in the *Oxford English Dictionary* comes from classical mythology and refers to a god or spirit who is assigned to watch over and guide an individual; it later came to mean "a person who powerfully influences for good or evil the character, conduct, or fortunes of another." Perhaps this is the most appropriate kind of "genius" to look for in this book. It is, at any rate, more accurate to my approach in compiling the book, for although I did seek out quotations by certain people as likely sources of wisdom, for the most part I was looking for words that might have an influence, rather than presuming to judge the native ability of the author.

On the other hand, I do hope that admiration for the quality of genius that created the passages quoted here will be one result of reading them. Unfortunately, many of these quotations don't do justice to the author's thought. All quotation distorts to some extent simply by the act of taking some words and leaving others, and with tight limitations on space, it is inevitable that you are not getting the full meaning of most, if not all, of these ideas. It is to be hoped that you get the ideas in a more concentrated and therefore more useful form, and that the additional layers of meaning created by bringing the ideas together compensate in some measure for what is lost from the original sources. Yet if I could hope for just one effect that this book would have on you, perhaps it would be that you might seek out some of these authors and read more of their work.

It's a curious thing how often certain ideas have been expressed. As Terence said over two thousand years ago, "Nothing is said that has not been said before"—and Goethe, among others, proved him right by saying it again in his own way some eighteen centuries later. But Goethe adds a useful suggestion for benefiting from this phenomenon; he says, "All truly wise thoughts have been thought already, thousands of times, but to make them truly ours, we must think them over again honestly, till they take firm root in our personal experience." That is what I hope you will do with these quotes.

And will they change your life? Do words ever really change our lives? That's an old debate, one on which a whole separate book of quotations could be compiled. I believe that they do in a sense. Words that actually changed things themselves would be magic spells; in the world of natural cause and effect, words, like so many other things, work indirectly.

These words of true genius can change your mind, your heart, and your choices if you let them—but many forces can interfere, including your own habitual thoughts and actions. So it is truer to say that the quotations in this book, with luck, can serve as a catalyst, but as for changing your life: reader, I leave that up to you.

1

LIFE IN THE UNIVERSE

Genius is a promontory jutting out of the infinite.

Victor Hugo

What are we doing here in the universe, and what's it all about? What is life, and does it have a meaning?

The quotes in this chapter are intended primarily to evoke thought or feelings that may in turn affect your life. They come from sages and scientists, poets and priests, and an assortment of other people who have something to say about the nature and meaning of human existence. Some of these quotes come from sacred texts, others from atheists. My hope is that many of them will carry their meanings across the lines of religious affiliation—and if not, there are plenty of other quotes for you to mull over.

I make no promise that this chapter will answer all of the questions mentioned above (even our quotable geniuses seem to shy away from a task that daunting!), but often it's enough just to raise the questions. Most of us spend most of our lives thinking about our immediate needs—a necessary perspective, but a limiting one. To step back and ponder the bigger picture once in a while is to awaken a faculty that is quintessentially human, and to open ourselves to being a little bit more than we were before.

The usual approach of science of constructing a mathematical model cannot answer the questions of why there should be a universe for the model to describe. Why does the universe go to all the bother of existing?

—Stephen Hawking, *A Brief History of Time: From the Big Bang to Black Holes*

Neither is there a smallest part of what is small, but there is always a smaller (for it is impossible that what is should cease to be). Likewise there is always something larger than what is large.

—Anaxagoras, pre-Socratic Greek philosopher

Our life is an apprenticeship to the truth, that around every circle another can be drawn; that there is no end in nature, but every end is a beginning; that there is always another dawn risen on mid-noon, and under every deep a lower deep opens.

—Ralph Waldo Emerson, *Essays*

There is no bliss in anything finite.
Infinity only is bliss.
The Infinite rests in its own greatness.

—*Chandogya Upanishad, Prapathaka*, Hindu scripture

In the plan of the Great Dance plans without number interlock, and each movement becomes in its season the breaking into flower of the whole design to which all else had been directed.

—C. S. Lewis, *Perelandra*

We are a way for the cosmos to know itself.

—Carl Sagan on Cosmos, quoted in *Rolling Stone*

We are not human beings having a spiritual experience; we are spiritual beings having a human experience.

—Pierre Teilhard de Chardin, French philosopher

It takes three things to attain a sense of significant being:

God
A Soul
And a moment.
And the three are always here.
Just to be is a blessing. Just to live is holy.

—Abraham Joshua Heschel, Polish-born American theologian

To live is so startling it leaves little time for anything else.

—Emily Dickinson

To live is the rarest thing in the world.
Most people exist, that is all.

—Oscar Wilde, *The Soul of Man*

I think I'm here for a purpose.
I think it's likely we all are,
but I'm only sure about myself.

—Jim Henson

Every man has been made by God
in order to acquire knowledge and contemplate.

—Pythagoras

Loving one another is our only reason for being.

—Dolly Parton, *My Life and Other Unfinished Business*

Life is the art of drawing without an eraser.

—John Christian, quoted in *Reader's Digest*

Life is a verb!

—Charlotte Perkins Gilman

Life is a quarry, out of which we are to mold
and chisel and complete a character.

—Johann Wolfgang von Goethe

Life is the art of drawing sufficient conclusions from insufficient premises.

—Samuel Butler, *Notebooks*

Life is a tragedy full of joy.

—Bernard Malamud, as quoted in *New York Times* January 1979

Life is a screen which separates us from the mystery of things.

—Victor Hugo, *Les Misérables*

Realize that life is glorious, and that you have no business taking it for granted. Care so deeply about its goodness that you want to spread it around.

—Anna Quindlen, *A Short Guide to a Happy Life*

I don't want to live. I want to love first, and live incidentally.

—Zelda Fitzgerald

All animals except man know that the principal business of life is to enjoy it.

—Samuel Butler, *Notebooks*

The purpose of life is not to be happy, but to matter.

—Leo Rosten

Socrates had it wrong; it is not the unexamined but finally the
uncommitted life that is not worth living.

—William Sloane Coffin

While I enjoy the friendship of the seasons
I trust that nothing can make life a burden to me.

—Henry David Thoreau, *Walden*

Living is like licking honey off a thorn.

—Louis Adamic

Everything lies in the moral courage with
which the apparent injustice of life
is faced and mastered.

—José Martí

I like living. I have sometimes been wildly, despairingly, acutely miserable,
racked with sorrow, but through it all I still know quite certainly that just
to be alive is a grand thing.

—Agatha Christie

There will always be something worth living for while there are shimmery afternoons.

—Olive Schreiner, *The Story of an African Farm*

Life is better than death, I believe, if only because it is less boring, and because it has fresh peaches in it.

—Alice Walker, in a speech at Grace Cathedral, San Francisco, March 16, 1982

Without music, life would be a mistake…
I would only believe in a God that knew how to dance.

—Friedrich Nietzsche

Music is essentially useless, as life is.

—George Santayana

Life is a gamble at terrible odds—if it was a bet,
you wouldn't take it.

—Tom Stoppard

The question, 'Is life worth living?' has been much discussed; particularly by those who think it is not, many of whom have written at great length in support of their view and by careful observance of the laws of health enjoyed for long terms of years the honors of successful controversy.

—Ambrose Bierce, *The Devil's Dictionary*

To live is like to love—all reason is against it, and all healthy instinct is for it.

—Samuel Butler, *Notebooks*

Believe that life is worth living, and your belief
will help create the fact.

—William James

If life has no meaning, why shouldn't we create a meaning for it?
Perhaps it's a mistake for us to look for meaning in this world, precisely
because our primary mission here is to create this meaning.

—Naguib Mahfouz, *Sugar Street*

Since man cannot help seeking the infinite, he now
seeks the meaning of his life in an infinity of things.

—Emil Brunner, *The Divine Imperative*

Is it so small a thing to have enjoyed the sun, to have lived light in the spring, to have loved, to have thought, to have done?

—Matthew Arnold

Life is to be lived,
not controlled, and humanity is won
by continuing to play
in face of certain defeat.

—Ralph Ellison

Clinton: I believe that life is for living, don't you?
Sebastien: It's difficult to know what else one could do with it.

—Noël Coward, *Nude with Violin*

A just conception of life is too large a thing to grasp during the short interval of passing through it.

—Thomas Hardy

The love of life is necessary to the vigorous prosecution of any undertaking.

—Samuel Johnson, *The Rambler*

Faith is the great motive power, and no man realizes his full possibilities unless he has the deep conviction that life is eternally important, and that his work, well done, is a part of an unending plan.

—Calvin Coolidge, in a speech in Washington, D.C., July 25, 1924

I care about life, but then there are things I care about more than life. For that reason I will not seek life improperly.

—Mencius

He who has a why to live for can bear almost any how.

—Friedrich Nietzsche

The struggle itself toward the heights is enough to fill a man's heart.
One must imagine Sisyphus happy.

—Albert Camus, referring to the struggle of the mythological figure who was condemned to roll a stone to the top of a hill, only to have it roll to the bottom again every time he reached the top

Perhaps the best I can do is to pray that the youth of today will have the **ability** to live simply and to get joy out of living, the **desire** to give of themselves and to make themselves worthy of giving, and the **strength** to do without anything which does not serve the interests of the brotherhood of man.

—Eleanor Roosevelt, "What I Hope to Leave Behind," in *Pictorial Review*

The art of living is not best understood by highly industrialized communities, where men are too busy to think, and where the cult of efficiency makes them reluctant to waste time, as they put it, by considering whether their standards of value correspond with the nature of things and with their own best selves.

—William Ralph Inge, Dean of St. Paul's Cathedral

Our inventions are . . . but improved means to an unimproved end, an
end which it was already but too easy to arrive at.

—Henry David Thoreau, *Walden*

It is very easy for us to get lost in the mundane world
and forget about our connection to spirit. Yet without that connection we
are basically the walking dead.

—Sobonfu Somé

Oh that man would seek immortal moments!
Oh that man would converse with God!

—William Blake

The most direct means for attaching ourselves to God from this material world is through music and song. Even if you can't sing well, sing. Sing to yourself. Sing in the privacy of your own home. But sing.

—Nachman of Bratslav

Music is the soul of life asking each of us to join its chorus.

—Marva N. Collins

All one's life is music, if one touches the notes rightly, and in time.

—John Ruskin

Joy comes from God. Who could live and who could breathe if the joy of Brahman filled not the universe? . . . from joy all beings have come and unto joy they all return.

—*Taittiriya Upanishad*

Joy is not in things; it is in us.

—Richard Wagner

Every name imposed by us onto God falls short of God. . . . God is inaccessible light, surpassing every light that can be seen by us either through sense or through intellect.

—Thomas Aquinas

We have created man, and we know what his soul whispers within him, for we are nearer to him than his jugular vein.

—The Koran, *50, 15*

Nobody is worthy to be loved. The fact that God loves man shows us that in the divine order of ideal things it is written that eternal love is to be given to what is eternally unworthy.

—Oscar Wilde, *De Profundis*

Dwelling deep within our hearts and the hearts of all beings without exception, is an inexhaustible source of love and wisdom. And the ultimate purpose of all spiritual practices . . . is to make contact with this essentially pure nature.

—Lama Thubten Yeshe

He who loves brings God and the world together.

—Martin Buber, *At the Turning*

The world will never starve for want of wonders; but only for want of wonder.

—G. K. Chesterton, *Tremendous Trifles*

Wonder . . . is essentially an 'opening' attitude—an awareness that there is more to life than one has yet fathomed, an experience of new vistas in life to be explored as well as new profundities to be plumbed.

—Rollo May

The divine Force, which inhabits every being,
every thing,
every place,
may be intensely realized when
man takes the trouble to invite it to reveal itself.

—Alassane Ndaw

God passes through the thicket of the world, and wherever his glance falls he turns all things to beauty.

—John of the Cross, Spanish Carmelite mystic

Most people in our culture
suppress their reactions
to beauty; it is too soul-baring.

—Rollo May

I have a terrible need of—shall I say the word—religion.
Then I go out and paint the stars.

—Vincent Van Gogh

The most beautiful thing we can experience is the mysterious. It is the source of all true art and science. He to whom this emotion is a stranger, who can no longer pause to wonder and stand rapt in awe, is as good as dead: his eyes are closed.

—Albert Einstein

I have long thought that anyone who does not regularly gaze up and see the wonder and glory of a dark night sky filled with countless stars loses a sense of their fundamental connectedness to the universe.

—Brian Greene

There is no question that the elegance of the universe is one of its most remarkable properties.

—Carl Sagan to Edward Wakin "God and Carl Sagan: Is the Cosmos Big Enough for Both of Them?, " *U.S. Catholic*, May 1981

The heavens declare the glory of God:
and the firmament sheweth his handiwork.

—Psalms 19:1

The morning wind forever blows,
the poem of creation is uninterrupted;
but few are the ears that hear it.
Olympus is but the outside of the earth everywhere.

—Henry David Thoreau, *Walden*

The happiest man is he who
learns from nature the lesson of worship.

—Ralph Waldo Emerson

If objects for gratitude and admiration are our desire, do they not present themselves every hour to our eyes? Do we not see a fair creation prepared to receive us the instant we were born—a world furnished to our hands that cost us nothing?

—Thomas Paine, *Age of Reason*

Gratitude is heaven itself.

—William Blake

Heaven is not a place, and it is not a time. Heaven is being perfect.

—Richard Bach, *Jonathan Livingston Seagull*

Seek not afar for beauty; lo, it glows
In dew-wet grasses all about your feet
In birds, in sunshine, childish faces sweet,
In stars and mountain summits topped with snows.

—Minot Judson Savage

All my life through, the new sights of Nature made me rejoice like a child.

—Marie Curie, *Pierre Curie*

Happy is the man who loves the woods and waters,
Brother to the grass, and well-beloved of Pan.

—Richard Le Gallienne

In those vernal seasons of the year when the air is soft and pleasant, it were an injury and sullenness against nature not to go out and see her riches, and partake of her rejoicings with heaven and earth.

—John Milton

Each beautiful thing, a flower, the song of a bird, awakens in our soul the memory of our origin. **Learn how to listen to the voice of beautiful things**, to make us understand the voice of our soul.

—from the Mevlevi Dervishes

The blue sky, the flower, the river, the cloud, these things have a healing nature... **We should allow ourselves to be healed**, and therefore, we should allow ourselves to be in the heart of life, which contains so many wonderful things, like the children, the flower, and so on.

—Thich Nhat Hahn

I think that's what life is all about actually—
about children and flowers.

—Audrey Hepburn

There is an experience of being in pure consciousness which gives lasting peace to the soul. It is an experience of the Ground or Depth of being in the Centre of the soul, an awareness of the mystery of being beyond sense and thought, which gives a sense of fulfillment, of finality, of absolute truth.

—Bede Griffiths, *Return to the Centre*

Though all is constantly changing, nothing is lost in the universe. Everything is connected to everything else by the iron law of cause and effect. Perhaps there is only one sin— **separateness**—with the blessedness of love making all whole.

—Helen Nearing, *Loving and Leaving the Good Life*

I never knew how to worship until I knew how to love.

—Henry Ward Beecher

Only by love can men see me, and know me,
and come unto me.

—*Bhagavad Gita* (translated by J. Mascaro, 1978)

All human love is a holy thing, the holiest thing in our experience.

—William Ralph Inge, Dean of St. Paul's Cathedral

If anything is sacred the human body is sacred.

—Walt Whitman, *I Sing the Body Electric*

The greatest beauty is organic wholeness, the wholeness of life and things, the divine beauty of the universe. Love that, not man apart from that.

—Robinson Jeffers, "The Answer"

To live we must daily break the body and shed the blood of Creation. When we do this **lovingly, knowingly, skillfully, reverently**, it is a sacrament. When we do it greedily, clumsily, ignorantly, destructively, it is a desecration. By such desecration we condemn ourselves to spiritual and moral loneliness and others to want.

—Wendell Berry, *Sierra*

We suffer yearnings without number that they may lead us to the yearning after which there is no yearning, so love God and He will make everything superfluous to you.

—Naguib Mahfouz, *Arabian Nights and Days*

When I cease searching and striving, I am always surprised to discover the density and meaningfulness, almost radiance, that ordinary things and actions have.

—Sam Keen, *To a Dancing God: Notes of a Spiritual Traveler*

Miracles, in the sense of phenomena we cannot explain, surround us on every hand: **life itself is the miracle of miracles.**

—George Bernard Shaw

There is grandeur in this view of life, with its several powers, having been originally breathed by the Creator into a few forms or into one; and that . . . from so simple a beginning endless forms most beautiful and most wonderful have been, and are being, evolved.

—Charles Darwin, *The Origin of Species*

That only which we have within, can we see without. If we meet no gods, it is because we harbor none. If there is grandeur in you, you will find grandeur in porters and sweeps. He only is rightly immortal, to whom all things are immortal.

—Ralph Waldo Emerson, "Worship," *The Conduct of Life*

And when not a bone or a tooth of my people survives, you, you will live on. You, my earth. No one will conquer you. No one will kill you.

—Driss Chraïbi, Moroccan writer

2

IDENTITY AND THE SELF

The sign of genius is the power of recognizing and assimilating that which is necessary to the development of oneself.

George Moore, *Evelyn Innes*

In the first chapter we considered life as an abstraction; now it's time to narrow the focus and think about your life. The one indispensable component of your life is you, so let's start there.

We use one of the two shortest words in the English language to refer to ourselves, but a self can be a pretty complex thing. What makes you who you are? How much is a given, a self-existent fact? How much comes from what has happened to you? How much of who you are is your own creation, deliberate or accidental?

None of us can tease out these threads from each other completely. But the following quotes offer some different perspectives on the weaving process, and may help us alter the pattern of the cloth.

You'll notice a great deal of disagreement within this chapter in the attitude toward the self. That disagreement is intentional; I believe that the best way to read the chapter is not to keep score, but rather to watch for the spin each speaker puts on the ball as he or she hits it, showing us a different face of the truth.

I believe that we cannot live better than in seeking to become better, nor more agreeably than having a clear conscience.

—Socrates

Man's main task in life is to give birth to himself, to become what he potentially is. The most important product of his effort is his own personality.

—Erich Fromm, *Man for Himself*

Human nature is not a machine to be built after a model, and set to do exactly the work prescribed for it, but a tree, which requires to grow and develop itself on all sides, according to the tendency of the inward forces which make it a living thing.

—John Stuart Mill, *On Liberty*

The purpose of all the major religious traditions is not to construct big temples on the outside, but to create temples of goodness and compassion inside, in our hearts.

—Tenzin Gyatso, the Fourteenth Dalai Lama

I believe that our fundamental task as human beings, persons, is to grow a soul, to develop our spiritual natures.

—W. Edward Harris

I have fought and kicked and fasted and prayed and cursed and cried myself to the point of existing. It has been like being born again, literally. Just knowing has meant everything to me. Knowing has pushed me out into the world, into college, into places, into people.

—Alice Walker

You are more than a human being,
you are a human **becoming**.

—Ann Harris

It is man's duty to forge a oneness
out of the manifoldness of his soul.

—Hans Kohn, *Die politische Idee des Judentums*

It takes courage to grow up and turn out to be
who you really are.

—e. e. cummings

We are what we pretend to be,
so we must be careful about
what we pretend to be.

—Kurt Vonnegut, Jr., in an interview in 2006

You mold your own life by the nature of the words
you speak;
and remember, you hear every word you speak.

—W. Edward Harris

What you are is God's gift to you;
what you make of yourself is your
gift to God.

—George Washington Carver

We all grow up with the weight of history on us. Our ancestors
dwell in the attics of our brains as they do in the spiraling chains of
knowledge hidden in every cell of our bodies.

—Shirley Abbott

One of the greatest things in life is that no one has the authority to tell you what you want to be. **You're the one who'll decide what you want to be.**

—Jaime Escalante

Not standing up on the bus that night was a matter of self-respect. Every day of my life, I have wanted to be treated with respect, and I have wanted to treat others with respect.

—Rosa Parks, on the Montgomery bus boycott

Every time you take the opportunity to speak from your deep convictions, you will learn more about yourself.

—Susan Partnow, *Everyday Speaking*

In matters of principle, stand like a rock;
in matters of taste, swim with the current.

—Thomas Jefferson

Any man worth his salt will stick up for what he believes right, but it takes a slightly better man to acknowledge instantly and without reservation that he is in error.

—Andrew Jackson

A man should never be ashamed to own he has been in the wrong, which is but saying, in other words, that he is wiser today than he was yesterday.

—Alexander Pope, *Thoughts on Various Subjects*

The trouble with most of us is that we would rather be ruined by praise than saved by criticism.

—Norman Vincent Peale

Labor to keep alive in your breast that little spark of celestial fire called conscience.

—from George Washington's maxims, *The Rules of Civility & Decent Behavior in Company and Conversation*

One trouble with guilt is that it often seeks punishment in order to avoid judgment; for while judgment demands a new way of life, punishment, by assuaging a bit the guilt, makes the old bearable anew.

—William Sloane Coffin

True guilt is guilt at the obligation one owes to oneself to be oneself. False guilt is guilt felt at not being what other people feel one ought to be or assume that one is.

—R. D. Laing, Scottish psychiatrist

I have a lot of things to prove to myself.
One is that I can live my life fearlessly.
But I don't have anything to prove to the world.

—Oprah Winfrey

It is better to be hated for what you are than to be loved for what you are not.

—André Gide

Each man is good in the sight of the Great Spirit.
It is not necessary for eagles to be crows.

—Sitting Bull

Never try to make anyone like you:
you know, and God knows,
that one of you is enough.

—Ralph Waldo Emerson

God creates each soul differently, so that when all the mud is finally cleared away, His light will shine through it in a beautiful, colorful, totally new pattern.

—M. Scott Peck, *People of the Lie*

There is no other task but to know your own original face. This is called independence; the spirit is clear and free. . . . Just look into your heart; there is a transcendental clarity. Just have no greed and no dependency and you will immediately attain certainty.

—Yen-t'ou, Zen master

Let us be grateful to the mirror for revealing to us
our appearance only.

—Samuel Butler, *Erewhon*

Looking foolish does the spirit good.

—John Updike

There is much to support the view that it is clothes that wear us and not we them; we may make them take the mould of arm or breast, but they would mould our hearts, our brains, our tongues to their liking.

—Virginia Woolf

Be careless in your dress if you will, but keep a tidy soul.

—Mark Twain

People wish to be settled. It is only as far as they are unsettled that there is any hope for them.

—Ralph Waldo Emerson, journal entry written in 1840

Habit is habit, and not to be flung out of the window by any man,
but coaxed downstairs a step at a time.

—Mark Twain, *Pudd'nhead Wilson's Calendar*

A bad habit never disappears miraculously;
it's an undo-it-yourself project.

—Abigail Van Buren

You would rather hope for goodness tomorrow than
practice it today.

—Marcus Aurelius, *Meditations*

How do we become true and good, happy and genuine, joyful and free? Never by magic, never by chance, never by sitting and waiting, but only by getting in touch with good, true, happy, genuine human beings ... only catching spontaneity and freedom from those who are themselves spontaneous and free.

—Charles Malik, as quoted in *Reader's Digest*, August 1972

The best rules to form a young man are:
to talk little
to hear much
to reflect alone upon what has passed in company
to distrust one's own opinions, and value others that deserve it.

–Sir William Temple

There is always one true inner voice. Trust it.

—Gloria Steinem

The most profound relationship we'll ever have is the one with ourselves.

—Shirley MacLaine

If we are such bad company that we can't live with ourselves, something is seriously wrong ... for sooner or later we shall have to face ourselves alone.

—Laura Ingalls Wilder

How essential it is ... to be able to live inside a mind with attractive and interesting pictures on the walls.

—William Lyon Phelps

All men who have turned out worth anything have had the chief hand in their own education.

—Sir Walter Scott

What, then, is true education?
It is awakening a love for truth, a just sense of duty,
opening the eyes of the soul to the great purpose and end of life.

—David O. McKay

The great end of education is, to discipline rather than to furnish the mind; to train it to the use of its own powers, rather than fill it with the accumulations of others.

—Tryon Edwards

Real learning comes not so much from reasonable thinking, but from those illuminating moments that permanently warp the mind.

—Henry Adams

It's what you learn after you know it all that counts.

—Earl Weaver, Baltimore Orioles manager

Learning, children would also forget. Would what they would learn be worth as much as what they would forget? I should like to ask you: can one learn this without forgetting that, and is what one learns worth what one forgets?

—Cheikh Hamidou Kane

Education is what survives when
what has been learned
has been forgotten.

—B. F. Skinner

It is always safe to learn, even from our enemies—
seldom safe to instruct, even our friends.

—Charles Caleb Colton, *Lacon*

Everything that irritates us about others
can lead us to an understanding of ourselves.

—Carl Jung

How can we learn self-knowledge? Never by taking thought but rather by
action. Try to do your duty and you'll soon discover what you're like.

—Johann Wolfgang von Goethe, *Wilhelm Meister's Journeyman Years*

If by gaining knowledge we destroy our health, we labour for a thing that will be useless in our hands.

—John Locke

A bow kept taut will quickly break, kept loosely strung, it will serve you when you need it.

—Phaedrus

A man too busy to take care of his health is like a mechanic too busy to take care of his tools.

—Spanish proverb

I have never yet met a healthy person who worried
very much about his health, or a really good person
who worried much about his own soul.

—J. B. S. Haldane, *Adventures of a Biologist*

The part can never be well unless the whole is well . . . For this is
the great error of our day in the treatment of the human body, that
physicians separate the soul from the body.

—Plato, *Dialogues*

Great thanks are due to Nature for putting into the life of each being so much healing power.

—Johann Wolfgang von Goethe

Above all, do not lose your desire to walk. Every day I walk myself into a state of well-being and walk away from every illness. I have walked myself into my best thoughts, and I know of no thought so burdensome that one cannot walk away from it.

—Sören Kierkegaard

Reading is to the mind what exercise is to the body.

—Joseph Addison, *Tatler*

Read first the best books.
The important thing for you is not how much you know,
but the quality of what you know.

—Desiderius Erasmus

One day's exposure to mountains is better than a cartload of books.

—John Muir

We read books to find out who we are. What other people, real or imaginary, do and think and feel . . . is an essential guide to our understanding of what we ourselves are and may become.

—Ursula K. LeGuin, *The Language of the Night*

Poetry can tell us what human beings are.
It can tell us why we stumble and fall and how,
miraculously, we can stand up.

—Maya Angelou, as quoted in *The Independent*

Poetry will not teach us how to live well, but it will incite in us the wish to.

—David Constantine, *Poetry Review*

The stories people tell have a way of taking care of them. If stories come to you, care for them. And learn to give them away where they are needed. Sometimes a person needs a story more than food to stay alive.

—Barry López, *Crow and Weasel*

We need myths to get by. We need story; otherwise the tremendous randomness of experience overwhelms us. Story is what penetrates.

—Robert Coover

We are what we imagine. Our very existence consists in our imagination of ourselves . . . The greatest tragedy that can befall us is to go unimagined.

—N. Scott Momaday

To reject one's own experiences is to arrest one's own development. To deny one's own experiences is to put a lie into the lips of one's own life. It is no less than a denial of the Soul.

—Oscar Wilde, *De Profundis*

You never find yourself until you face the truth.

—Pearl Bailey, *The Raw Pearl*

We become evil by attempting to hide from ourselves.

—M. Scott Peck, *People of the Lie*

All evil is potential vitality in need of transformation.

—Sheldon B. Kopp, *If You Meet the Buddha on the Road, Kill Him!*

Once you have the courage to look upon evil, seeing it for what it is and naming it by its true name, it is powerless against you, and you can destroy it.

—Lloyd Alexander, *The Book of Three*

Annihilation itself is no death to evil.
Only good where evil was, is evil dead.

—George MacDonald, *Lilith*

In what way, or by what manner of working, God changes a soul from evil to good, how He impregnates the barren rock—the priceless gems and gold—is to the human mind an impenetrable mystery in all cases alike.

—Samuel Taylor Coleridge

Each of us is redeemed from shallow and hostile life
only by the sacrificial love and civility
which we have gratuitously received.

—Sam Keen, *To a Dancing God: Notes of a Spiritual Traveler*

Love is something you and I must have...

With it we are creative. With it we march tirelessly. With it, and with it alone, we are able to sacrifice for others.

—Chief Dan George

Therefore you should strive to think of all that lives with friendliness and compassion, and not with ill-will and a desire to hurt. For whatever a man thinks about continually, to that his mind becomes inclined by the force of habit.

—Siddhartha Gautama, the Buddha

When people will not weed their own minds,
they are apt to be overrun with nettles.

—Horace Walpole

The individual is capable of both great compassion and great
indifference. He has it within his means to nourish the former and
outgrow the latter.

—Norman Cousins

We are all of us born in moral stupidity,
taking the world as an udder to feed our supreme selves.

—George Eliot, *Middlemarch*

Since we desire the true happiness that is brought about by only a calm mind, and since such peace of mind is brought about by only a compassionate attitude, how can we develop this? . . . We must use all the events of our daily life to transform our thoughts and behavior.

—Tenzin Gyatso, the Fourteenth Dalai Lama

Oh! that I could wear out of my mind every mean and base affectation; conquer my natural pride and self-conceit; expect no more deference from my fellows than I deserve; acquire that meekness and humility which are the sure mark and characters of a great and generous soul; **subdue every unworthy passion, and treat all men as I wish to be treated by all.**

—from the diary of John Adams

We shall strive for perfection. We shall not achieve it immediately, but we still shall strive. We may make mistakes, but they must never be mistakes which result from faintness of heart or abandonment of moral principle.

—Franklin Delano Roosevelt, final inaugural address, January 20, 1945

We are the rocks we are pushing uphill.

—Judith Sills, *The Comfort Trap*

Have patience with all things, but chiefly have patience with yourself. Do not lose courage in considering your own imperfections, but instantly start remedying them—every day begin the task anew.

—St. Francis de Sales

The thing that is really hard, and really amazing, is giving up on being perfect and beginning the work of becoming yourself.

—Anna Quindlen

We are all serving a life-sentence in the dungeon of self.

—Cyril Connolly

Will not a tiny speck very close to our vision blot out the glory of the world, and leave only a margin by which we see the blot? **I know no speck so troublesome as self.**

—George Eliot, *Middlemarch*

When a man is wrapped up in himself,
he makes a pretty small package.

—John Ruskin

Prayer makes your heart bigger, until it is capable of containing the gift of God himself.

—Mother Teresa

There are so many gifts
Still unopened from your birthday,
There are so many hand-crafted presents
That have been sent to you by God.
The Beloved does not mind repeating,
'Everything I have is also yours,'
There are so many gifts, my dear,
Still unopened from your birthday.

—Hafiz

**Oh God, deliver me from this lust
of always justifying myself.**

—St. Augustine

Perhaps the only true dignity of man
is his capacity to despise himself.

—George Santayana

Be gentle with yourself.
You are a child of the universe,
no less than the trees and the stars.
In the noisy confusion of life, keep peace in your soul.

—Max Ehrmann

[Possessed] verily thou art, and grievously tormented. Shall I tell thee who hath possessed thee? . . . **His name is Self, and he is the shadow of thy own self.** First he made thee love him, which was evil, and now he hath made thee hate him, which is evil also. But if he be cast out and never more enter into thy heart, but remain as a servant in thy hall, then wilt thou … find the varlet serviceable.

—George MacDonald, *St. George and St. Michael*

My soul spake to me and said, 'The lantern which you carry is not yours, and the song that you sing was not composed within your heart, for even if you bear the light, you are not the light, and even if you are a lute fastened with strings, you are not the lute player.'

—Kahlil Gibran, "My Soul Counseled Me"

The one important thing I have learned over the years is the difference between taking one's work seriously and taking one's self seriously. The first is imperative and the second is disastrous.

—Margot Fonteyn

Integrate what you believe in every single area of your life. Take your heart to work and ask the most and best of everybody else, too. Don't let your special character and values, the secret that you know and no one else does, the truth—don't let that get swallowed up by the great chewing complacency.

—Meryl Streep

I'm finally ready to own my own power, to say
'This is who I am.'
If you like it, you like it.
And if you don't, you don't.
So watch out, I'm gonna fly.

—Oprah Winfrey

No bird soars too high, if he soars with his own wings.

—William Blake, *The Marriage of Heaven and Hell*

We have been raised to fear the **yes** in ourselves.

—Audre Lorde

Courage is the basic virtue for everyone
so long as he continues to grow,
to move ahead.

—Rollo May, *Man's Search for Himself*

We must learn the power of living with our helplessness.

—Sheldon B. Kopp, *If You Meet the Buddha on the Road, Kill Him!*

Our deepest fear is not that we are inadequate. **Our deepest fear is that we are powerful beyond measure.** It is our light, not our darkness, that most frightens us. We ask ourselves, Who am I to be brilliant, gorgeous, talented, fabulous? Actually, who are you not to be? You are a child of God.

—Marianne Williamson, *A Return to Love*

Those who stand at the threshold of life always waiting for the right time to change are like the man who stands at the bank of a river waiting for the water to pass so he can cross on dry land.

—Joseph B. Wirthlin

The inner self of every human waits patiently
until we are ready;
then it extends an invitation to enter
the luminous mystery of existence in which all things are created,
nurtured, and renewed.
In the presence of this mystery, we not only heal ourselves,
we heal the world.

—Deepak Chopra, *Power, Freedom and Grace: Living from the Source of Lasting Happiness*

3

CHARACTER AND PERSONAL ACTION

Genius is initiative on fire.

Holbrook Jackson

In this chapter we finally get to move past the subject and on to the verb. It's time for some action. Whoever this self of yours is, it's got to do something in order to change your life, and this chapter brings together some thoughts to get the ball rolling.

We won't move away from the self all at once, though. What we do is intimately connected to what we are, and the first part of the chapter is devoted to quotations about character and some of the virtues that constitute it.

From character we move on to a cluster of quotations about duty. The word "duty" is perhaps starting to sound a little old-fashioned—which is all the more reason we should hear about it sometimes. Perhaps in our times, with our emphasis on self-determination, we find our duty less clearly laid out for us than some of our ancestors. Maybe that means that we need to take more thought to discover it, or, if it's not a contradiction in terms to say this, to choose or create our duty.

Having accepted our duty—or chosen to do anything, whether it is a duty or not—we must take action and get to work on it. The rest of the chapter focuses on action and work, and illustrates some of the rewards and pitfalls associated with them.

Character is power.

—Booker T. Washington

Character is that which can do without success.

—Ralph Waldo Emerson, *Uncollected Lectures*

While I feel the most lively gratitude for the many instances of approbation from my country; I can no otherwise deserve it, than by obeying the dictates of my conscience.

—George Washington, to the Boston Selectmen, July 28, 1795

Conscience is thoroughly well-bred and soon leaves off talking to those who do not wish to hear it.

—Samuel Butler, *Further Extracts from Notebooks*

Men do not differ much about what things they will call evils; they differ enormously about what evils they will call excusable.

—G. K. Chesterton

But this is not difficult, O Athenians, to escape death, but it is
much more difficult to avoid depravity,
for it runs swifter than death.

—Socrates, from *Plato's Apology*

**The reason most people are bad
is because they do not try to be good.**

—L. Frank Baum, *The Emerald City of Oz*

Integrity is one of those words which many people
keep in that desk drawer labeled "too hard."

—James Bond Stockdale, "The World of Epictetus"

Live so that you wouldn't be ashamed
to sell the family parrot to the town gossip.

—Will Rogers

Goodness consists not in the outward things we do,
but in the inward thing we are.

—E. H. Chapin

A man is only as good as what he loves.

—Saul Bellow

Courage is rightly esteemed the first of human qualities,
because . . . it is the quality which guarantees all others.

—Winston Churchill, *Great Contemporaries*

A thankful heart is not only the greatest virtue,
but the parent of all the other virtues.

—Cicero

True humility is the low, but deep and firm foundation of all real virtue.

—Edmund Burke

To be vain of one's rank or place, is to show that one is below it.

—Stanislas I

Conceit is an outward manifestation of inferiority.

—Noël Coward

Humility does not mean you think less of yourself.
It means you think of yourself less.

—Dr. Kenneth Blanchard, American business consultant

Your honesty is not to be based either on religion or policy. Both your religion and policy must be based on it. Your honesty must be based, as the sun is, in vacant heaven; poised, as the lights in the firmament, which have rule over the day and over the night.

—John Ruskin, *Time and Tide*

**The most common lie is that with which
one lies to oneself:**
lying to others is relatively an exception.

—Friedrich Nietzsche

The universal conspiracy of the silent-assertion lie is hard at work always and everywhere, and always in the interest of a stupidity or a sham, never in the interest of a thing fine or respectable.

—Mark Twain, "My First Lie, and How I Got Out of It"

This excellent method of conveying a falsehood with the heart only, without making the tongue guilty of an untruth, by the means of equivocation and imposture, hath quieted the conscience of many a notable deceiver; and yet, when we consider that it is Omniscience on which these endeavor to impose, it may possibly seem capable of affording only a very superficial comfort; and that this artful and refined **distinction between communicating a lie, and telling one, is hardly worth the pains it costs them.**

—Henry Fielding, *Tom Jones*

The man who is brutally honest
enjoys the brutality quite as much
as the honesty.

—Richard J. Needham in *The Globe and Mail*, Toronto

**A man never discloses his own character so clearly
as when he describes another's.**

—Jean Paul

The true measure of a man is how he treats someone
who can do him absolutely no good.

—attributed to Samuel Johnson

For fidelity, devotion, love, many a two-legged animal is below the dog and the horse. Happy would it be for thousands of people if they could stand at last before the Judgment Seat and say 'I have loved as truly and I have lived as decently as my dog'.

—Henry Ward Beecher

Cruelty . . . argues not only a depravedness of nature, but also a meanness of courage and imbecility of mind.

—Sir William Temple

On the whole, my impression is that mercy bears
richer fruits than any other attribute.

—Abraham Lincoln

There is only one quality worse than hardness of heart,
and that is softness of head.

—Theodore Roosevelt

Human kindness has never weakened the stamina
or softened the fiber of a free people.
A nation does not have to be cruel to be tough.

—Franklin Delano Roosevelt

Wise sayings often fall on barren ground;
but a kind word is never thrown away.

—Sir Arthur Helps

When I was young I admired clever people.
Now that I am old, I admire kind people.

—Abraham Joshua Heschel

Ever since puberty I have believed in the value of two things:
kindness and clear thinking. Gradually, the two have come more and more
together in my feelings. I find that much unclear thought exists as an excuse
for cruelty, and that much cruelty is prompted by superstitious beliefs.

—Bertrand Russell

Kind hearts are the gardens. Kind thoughts are the roots. Kind words are the blossoms. Kind deeds are the fruits.

—Kirpal Singh

To be a man is, precisely, to be responsible.

—Antoine de Saint-Exupéry

I believe that every right implies a responsibility; every opportunity an obligation; every possession a duty.

—John D. Rockefeller, as quoted in *Time*, July 21, 1941

Every duty which we omit, obscures some truth which we should have known.

—John Ruskin

Every time we say 'I must do something'
it takes an incredible amount of energy.
Far more than physically doing it.

—Gita Bellin, American author and consultant

As we must account for every idle word,
so we must for every idle silence.

—Benjamin Franklin

[I]t is often easier to fight for principles than to live up to them.

—Adlai E. Stevenson, Jr.,
in a speech to the Democratic National Convention,
Chicago, Illinois, July 21, 1952

Each of our acts makes a statement as to our purpose.

— Leo Buscaglia

Duty then is the sublimest word in our language. Do your duty in all things. You cannot do more. You should never wish to do less.

—Robert E. Lee

It is awfully important to know what is and what is not your business.

—Gertrude Stein, "What is English Literature"

In my humble opinion, non-cooperation with evil is as much a duty as is cooperation with good.

—Mahatma Gandhi, from statement at trial for sedition in Madras, India, March 23, 1922

Perform your own duty first,
and then you will have right
to make other people perform theirs.

—Thomas Paine, "A Friend to Rhode Island and the Union", 1783

He who is slow in promising
is always the most faithful in performing.

—Jean-Jacques Rousseau

All glory comes from daring to begin.

—Eugene F. Ware

We cannot seek or attain health, wealth, learning, justice or kindness in general. Action is always specific, concrete, individualized, unique.

—John Dewey

Wisdom is knowing what to do next; **virtue is doing it.**

—David Starr Jordan, educator, scientist, and peace activist

Do what you can,
with what you have,
where you are.

—Theodore Roosevelt

If you travel the earth, you will find it is largely divided into two classes of people—people who say 'I wonder why such and such is not done' and people who say 'Now who is going to prevent me from doing that thing?'

—Winston Churchill

In every action reflect upon the end;
and in your undertaking it consider why you do it.

—Jeremy Taylor

Rhetoric is not important. Actions are.

—Nelson Mandela

Don't say that you want to give, but go ahead and give!
You'll never catch up with a mere hope.

—Johann Wolfgang von Goethe

I would wish to say that today is the day of compassion. Let's not wait to be prompted, but let us go out tonight, tomorrow and the days that follow, and let us demonstrate our humanity. **Let us not wait to be asked, but let us act today.**

—Princess Diana, speech at Humanitarian Awards Dinner, New York United Cerebral Palsy, December 11, 1995

The belief that God will do everything for man is as untenable as the belief that man can do everything for himself. It, too, is based on a lack of faith. We must learn that to expect God to do everything while we do nothing is not faith but superstition.

—Martin Luther King, Jr.

True proactiveness comes from seeing how
we contribute to our own problems.

—Peter Senge

Never let the fear of striking out get in your way.

—Babe Ruth

When it becomes necessary to do a thing,
the whole heart and soul
should go into the measure,
or not attempt it.

—Thomas Paine, *Rights of Man*

The oldest habit in the world for resisting change is to complain that unless the remedy to the disease can be universally applied it should not be applied at all. But you must begin somewhere.

—Winston Churchill, in a speech at House of Commons, May 15, 1911

A wise man will make more opportunities than he finds.

—Francis Bacon

If your ship doesn't come in, swim out to it.

—Jonathan Winters

Never mistake motion for action.

—Ernest Hemingway

He who does something at the head of one Regiment, will eclipse him who does nothing at the head of a hundred.

—Abraham Lincoln, to General David Hunter, who had complained because he was sent to Leavenworth and expected to command only 3,000 men there

I find that if I am thinking too much of my own problems and the fact that at times things are not just like I want them to be, I do not make any progress at all. But if I look around and see what I can do, and then I do it, I move on.

—Rosa Parks

Opportunity is missed by most people because it is
dressed in overalls and looks like work.

—Thomas A. Edison

The world is divided into people who do things
and people who get the credit.
Try, if you can, to belong to the first class.
There's far less competition.

—Dwight Morrow, letter to his son

The only way to enjoy life is to work.
Work is much more fun than fun.

—Noël Coward, from *Observer Sayings of the Week*

Happiness lies not in the mere possession of money; it lies in the joy of achievement, in the thrill of creative effort. The joy and moral stimulation of work no longer must be forgotten in the mad chase of evanescent profits.

—Franklin Delano Roosevelt, first inaugural address, March 4, 1933

Employment is nature's physician, and is essential to human happiness.

—Galen

The reward of labour is life. Is that not enough?

—William Morris, *News from Nowhere*

The highest reward for a man's toil is not what he gets for it, but what he becomes.

—John Ruskin

Perfect freedom is reserved for the man who lives by his own work
and in that work does what he wants to do.

—R. G. Collingwood, *Speculum Mentis*

The nearly intolerable irony in our dissatisfaction is that we have removed pleasure from our work in order to remove 'drudgery' from our lives. If I could pick any rule of industrial economics to receive a thorough re-examination by our people, it would be the one that says that all hard physical work is 'drudgery' and not worth doing.

—Wendell Berry, *What Are People For?*

Anyone can do any amount of work, provided it isn't the work he is supposed to be doing at the moment.

—Robert Benchley

He is not only idle who does nothing, but he is idle who might be better employed.

—Socrates

Where your talents and the needs
of the world cross lies your calling.

—Aristotle

Every man is born into the world to do something unique and something distinctive, and if he or she does not do it, it will never be done.

—Dr. Benjamin E. Mays

Blessed is he who has found his work;
let him ask no other blessedness.

—Thomas Carlyle, *Past and Present*

Vocations which we wanted to pursue, but didn't, bleed, like colors, on the whole of our existence.

—Honoré de Balzac

I wanted to be a theologian; for a long time I was unhappy. Now, behold, God is praised by my work even in astronomy.

— Johannes Kepler

To work is to pray.

—St. Benedict

A human being must have occupation if he or she is not to become a nuisance to the world.

—Dorothy L. Sayers

You cannot be really first-rate at your work
if your work is all you are.

—Anna Quindlen, *A Short Guide to a Happy Life*

One thing I would have dreaded would be to
look back on my life and only have movies.

—Audrey Hepburn

All true Work is sacred.

—Thomas Carlyle, *Past and Present*

The society which scorns excellence in plumbing as a humble activity and tolerates shoddiness in philosophy because it is an exalted activity will have neither good plumbing nor good philosophy: neither its pipes nor its theories will hold water.

—John W. Gardner

Resolve to be honest at all events; and if in your judgment you cannot be an honest lawyer, resolve to be honest without being a lawyer. Choose some other occupation, rather than one in the choosing of which you do, in advance, consent to be a knave.

—Abraham Lincoln, from notes taken
in preparation for a lecture on law, July 1, 1850

Make a career of humanity . . . and you will make a greater person of yourself, a greater nation of your country and a finer world to live in.

—Martin Luther King, Jr.

The world is full of willing people;
some willing to work,
the rest willing to let them.

—Robert Frost

**It's been my policy to do every job assigned to me
just a little better than anyone else has done it.**

—Harry S. Truman

**A professional is someone who can do his best work
when he doesn't feel like it.**

—Alistair Cooke

Besides the noble art of getting things done, there is the noble art of leaving things undone. The wisdom of life consists of the elimination of nonessentials.

—Lin Yutang

It is better to wear out than to rust out.

—Bishop Richard Cumberland

The main thing, Ruby said, was not to get ahead of yourself. Go at a rhythm that could be sustained on and on. **Do just as much as you could do and still be able to get up and do again tomorrow.** No more, and no less.

—Charles Frazier, *Cold Mountain*

If you could once make up your mind never to undertake more work . . . than you can carry on calmly, quietly, without hurry or flurry . . . and if the instant you feel yourself growing nervous . . . you would stop and take breath, you would find this simple common-sense rule doing for you what no prayers or tears could ever accomplish.

—Elizabeth Prentiss

4

TRUTH

True genius resides in the capacity for evaluation of uncertain, hazardous, and conflicting information.

Winston Churchill

"What is truth?" Pilate reportedly asked Jesus just before Jesus was crucified, and surely there has seldom been a greater disparity between the size of a question and the time allotted for its answer. Truth is a big thing to try to get our minds around, and a tricky subject to discuss in a world full of disagreement at some of the most fundamental levels. But our notions of what is true, and the degree of our commitment to truth, underlie our choices. So thinking about truth really can change our lives.

As we begin to think about truth, many of us probably assume that truth ought to be objective, and therefore single: that there ought to be a Right Answer. Hence the passion with which people argue when their "right answers" disagree with each other. Some say that the notion of a single truth is too simple, that truth is subjective and hence multiple. However we choose to handle this question at the ultimate level, when we deal with individual statements of truth from any given human being it's clear that we are in subjective territory—that what a person sees as true depends on how he or she perceives things and thinks about them.

Thinking can be hard work, and truth can be scary or unpleasant. That should not deter us either from thinking or from trying to find and speak the truth. I hope that the quotations here serve to give all of us a nudge and lead to a little less shirking in this regard. And if not—well, we can always just use the quotations to shirk more effectively, as A. A. Milne suggests: "A quotation is a handy thing to have about, saving one from the trouble of thinking for oneself."

As soon as you can say what you think, and not what some other person has thought for you, you are on the way to being a remarkable man.

—Sir J. M. Barrie

Better keep yourself clean and bright;
you are the window through which
you must see the world.

—George Bernard Shaw

Our ideas, like orange-plants, spread out in proportion to the size of the box which imprisons the roots.

—Edward Bulwer-Lytton

Inevitably, **the culture within which we live shapes and limits our imaginations,** and by permitting us to do and think and feel in certain ways makes it increasingly unlikely or impossible that we should do or think or feel in ways that are contradictory or tangential to it.

—Margaret Mead

None of us can fully escape this blindness [of our own age], but we shall certainly increase it, and weaken our guard against it, if we read only modern books . . . The only palliative is to keep the clean sea breeze of the centuries blowing through our minds, and **this can be done only by reading old books.**

—C. S. Lewis, "On the Reading of Old Books," *God in the Dock* (originally the introduction to St. Athanasius's *The Incarnation of the Word of God*)

Pick the assumptions to pieces till
the stuff they are made of is exposed to plain view—
this is the cardinal rule for
understanding the basis of our beliefs.

—Eric T. Bell, *The Search for Truth*

A closed mind is a dying mind.

—Edna Ferber, radio broadcast, 1947

Let go of your attachment to being right, and suddenly your mind is more open. You're able to benefit from the unique viewpoints of others, without being crippled by your own judgment.

—Ralph Marston

If you keep your mind sufficiently open,
people will throw a lot of rubbish into it.

—William A. Orten

If you shut your door to all errors truth will be shut out.

—Rabindranath Tagore, *Stray Birds*

[T]he old law of the natural philosophers, that Nature abhors a vacuum, is true of the human head. . . . Therefore I warn you that **if you leave the smallest corner of your head vacant for a moment, other people's opinions will rush in from all quarters.**

—George Bernard Shaw, *The Intelligent Woman's Guide to Socialism, Capitalism, Sovietism & Fascism*

Everybody is ignorant, only on different subjects.

—Will Rogers

To prejudge other people's notions before we have looked into them is not to show their darkness but to put out our own eyes.

—John Locke

One had rather have no opinion than a false one.

—Thomas Jefferson, Memorandum, June 6, 1787

Children begin by honestly saying, 'I don't know,' until they are taught (mistakenly) to be ashamed of ignorance; and this is why so many adults remain ashamed of saying, 'I don't know' when they should say it. Ignorance is shameful only when we have had the opportunity to learn something and rejected it.

—Sydney J. Harris, *Pieces of Eight*

The worst thing we can do with a dilemma is to resolve it prematurely because we haven't the courage to live with uncertainty.

—William Sloane Coffin

The man who never alters his opinion
is like standing water,
and breeds reptiles of the mind.

—William Blake, *The Marriage of Heaven and Hell*

People see God every day; they just don't recognize him.

—Pearl Bailey, interview, *The New York Times*, Nov. 26, 1967

Attitudes have a kind of inertia. Once set in motion, they will keep going, even in the face of the evidence. To change an attitude requires a considerable amount of work and suffering. . . . It is only from the quicksand of confusion that we are able to leap to the new and better vision.

—M. Scott Peck, *The People of the Lie*

The world is God's epistle to mankind—
his thoughts are flashing upon
us from every direction.

—Plato

The moment one gives close attention to any thing, even a blade of
grass, it becomes a mysterious, awesome, indescribably magnificent
world in itself.

—Henry Miller

The best place to meditate is in the meadows outside the city.
One should meditate in a grassy field,
for grass will awaken the heart.

—Nachman of Bratzlav

It is only with the heart that one can see rightly;
what is essential is invisible to the eye.

—Antoine de Saint Exupéry, *The Little Prince*

Many people live in ugly wastelands but in the absence of
imaginative standards most of them do not even know it.

—C. Wright Mills, *Power, Politics, and People*

A strange lot this, to be dropped down in a world of barbarians—men who
see clearly enough the barbarity of all ages except their own.

—Ernest Crosby, *The Soul of the World*

Satire is a sort of glass in which beholders generally discover
everybody's face but their own.

—Jonathan Swift, *The Battle of the Books*

The injury we do and the one we suffer
are not weighed in the same scales.

—Aesop

Of course, it is easy to turn your eyes from what is happening
if it is not happening to you. Or if you have not
put yourself where it is happening.

—Susan Sontag in *New York Times Magazine,* May 2, 1999

Idealism increases in direct proportion to one's
distance from the problem.

—John Galsworthy

I abandoned the bird's-eye view that lets you see everything from above, from the sky. I assumed a worm's-eye view, trying to find whatever comes right in front of you—smell it, touch it, see if you can do something about it.

—Muhammad Yunus, founder of Grameen Bank, winner of 2006 Nobel Peace Prize

Not only is there but one way of doing things rightly,
but there is only one way of seeing them, and that is,
seeing the whole of them.

—John Ruskin, *The Two Paths*

There are two spiritual dangers in not owning a farm. One is the danger of supposing that breakfast comes from the grocery, and the other that heat comes from the furnace.

—Aldo Leopold, *A Sand County Almanac*

Now in creative thought common sense is a bad master. Its sole criterion for judgment is that the new ideas shall look like the old ones. In other words it can only act by suppressing originality.

—Alfred North Whitehead, *An Introduction to Mathematics*

I have but one lamp by which my feet are guided, and that is the lamp of experience. I know of no way of judging of the future but by the past.

—Patrick Henry, speech to Virginia Convention of Delegates, March 28, 1775

[I]t is the privilege and proper condition of a human being, arrived at the maturity of his faculties, to use and interpret experience in his own way.

—John Stuart Mill, *On Liberty*

Experience is the great teacher;
unfortunately, experience leaves mental scars,
and scar tissue contracts.

—William J. Mayo, *Journal of the American Medical Association*

I hope you have developed some real intellectual curiosity.
If you have it you will never, never be bored. . . . To the intellectually curious the world will be full of magic and full of wonder.

—Majorie Pay Hinckley, address at Brigham Young University commencement April 20, 2000

I believe that in every person is a kind of circuit
which resonates to intellectual discovery—
and the idea is to make that resonance work.

—Carl Sagan to Dennis Meredith "Carl Sagan's Cosmic Connection and Extraterrestrial
Life-Wish," *Science Digest*, June 1979

It is . . . nothing short of a miracle that the modern methods of
instruction have not yet entirely strangled the holy curiosity of
inquiry; for this delicate little plant, aside from stimulation, stands
mainly in need of freedom; without this it goes to wreak and ruin.

—Albert Einstein

The desire of knowledge, like the thirst of riches, increases ever with the acquisition of it.

—Laurence Sterne, *Tristram Shandy*

Some people drink from the fountain of knowledge,
others just gargle.

—Robert Anthony

You have to drill through mud and water to get oil; you have to sift through sand and silt to get gold; you have to chop and hack through stone to get diamonds. So why do so many people feel that the treasure of ideas should come to them with little or no effort?

—Sydney J. Harris, *Pieces of Eight*

Almost every man tries to dodge thought or to find a substitute for it. We try to buy thoughts ready made and guaranteed to fit, in the shape of systems installed by experts. We try to substitute discussion for thought a spell spent in talking [is not the same as] a spell spent in thinking.

—Harvey Firestone

Think, think, think.
It will hurt like hell at first, but you'll get used to it.

—Barbara Castle, British politician

I don't think thinking about a situation does much good.
One knows by instinct what one can do.

—A. C. Benson,
Excerpts from *Letters of Dr. A. C. Benson to M. E. A.*

**You can't depend on your judgment when
your imagination is out of focus.**

—Mark Twain, *Mark Twain Papers*

More life may trickle out of men through thought
Than through a gaping wound.

—Thomas Hardy

A great many people think they are thinking
when they are merely rearranging their prejudices.

—William James

The fact that an [opinion] has been widely held is no evidence
whatever that it is not utterly absurd.

—Bertrand Russell

I am never easy now, when I am handling a thought, till I have bounded it
north and bounded it south, and bounded it east and bounded it west.

—Abraham Lincoln, quoted in *The New York Independent,* September 1, 1864

The true, strong and sound mind is the mind
that can embrace equally great things and small.

—Samuel Johnson, quoted in *The Life of Samuel Johnson* by James Boswell

I do not feel obliged to believe that the same God who endowed us with sense, reason, and intellect intended us to forgo their use.

—Galileo

It is that which we do know which is the great hindrance to our learning that which we do not know.

—Claude Bernard
An Introduction to the Study of Experimental Medicine

A sedentary life is the real sin against the Holy Spirit. Only those thoughts that come by walking have any value.

—Friedrich Nietzsche, "Maxims and Missiles"

Men occasionally stumble over the truth, but most of them pick themselves up and hurry off as if nothing had happened.

—Winston Churchill

The best way to have a good idea is to have a lot of ideas.

—Linus Pauling, Nobel Prize winner in chemistry

It is better to know some of the questions than all of the answers.

—James Thurber

There is one thing stronger than all the armies of the world;
and that is an idea whose time has come.

—Victor Hugo

A new idea is delicate.
It can be killed by a sneer or a yawn;
it can be stabbed to death by a joke
or worried to death by a frown
on the right person's brow.

—Charles Browder

It is of the nature of idea to be communicated: written, spoken, done. The idea is like grass. It craves light, likes crowds, thrives on crossbreeding, grows better for being stepped on.

—Ursula K. LeGuin, *The Dispossessed: An Ambiguous Utopia*

It does not require many words to speak the truth.

—Chief Joseph

Truth is violated by falsehood, but it is outraged by silence.

—Henri Frederic Amiel

I am very little inclined on any occasion to say anything unless I hope to produce some good by it.

—Abraham Lincoln, quoted in *Harper's Weekly*, August 23, 1862

It is rarely possible to carry the torch of truth through a crowd without singeing somebody's beard.

—Joshua Bruyn

To comprehend with your heart what your mind cannot fathom is the beginning of understanding.

—Perry A. White, *Reflections*

Your vision will become clear only when you look into your heart. Who looks outside, dreams. Who looks inside, awakens.

—Carl Jung

There's nothing like eavesdropping to show you that the world outside
your head is different from the world
inside your head.

—Thornton Wilder, *The Matchmaker*

Learning without wisdom is a load of books on a donkey's back.

—Zora Neale Hurston

Nine-tenths of wisdom is being wise in time.

—Theodore Roosevelt, as quoted in *Kansas City Star*, November 1, 1917

Man passes away; generations are but shadows;
there is nothing stable but truth.

—Josiah Quincy, Jr., President of Harvard University,
in a speech in Boston, September 17, 1830

Truth is a rock; if you chip away at it enough, you wind up with gravel,
then sand.

—Anna Quindlen, "Real Life, No Police Chases," *Newsweek*, January 23, 2006

I do not mind lying, but I hate inaccuracy.

—Samuel Butler, *Notebooks*

Creation not only exists, it also discharges truth . . . Wisdom requires a surrender, verging on the mystical, of a person to the glory of existence.

—Gerhard von Rad, German biblical scholar

The reason we do not see truth is not that we have not read enough books or do not have enough academic degrees, but that we do not have enough courage.

—Rollo May

Be ye lamps unto yourselves; be your own confidence; hold to the truth within yourselves as to the only lamp.

—attributed to Siddhartha Gautama, the Buddha, 5th c. BCE

That type of obedience, where you find refuge in the corporate, or where you find refuge in the political or religious majority, is such an absolutely despicable cowardice. . . . I think that every time you turn towards a truth that is not your own, that you confide the guidance of your soul to somebody else's choices, you are making a huge mistake.

—Guillermo del Toro, director of *Pan's Labyrinth*, in an interview with Terry Gross, *Fresh Air*, January 24, 2007

The presence of those seeking the truth is infinitely to be preferred to those who think they've found it.

—Terry Pratchett

The pretensions of final truth are always partly an effort to obscure a darkly felt consciousness of the limits of human knowledge.

—Reinhold Niebuhr, U.S. theologian

Those who believe that they are exclusively in the right are generally those who achieve something.

—Aldous Huxley, *Proper Studies*

The greatest disorder of the mind is to let will direct belief.

—Louis Pasteur

I'm not seeking the truth—nor was I ever.
I was born knowing the truth. Everybody is.
Trouble is they get it knocked out of them
before they can walk.

—Bob Dylan

The word of God is the secret word. He who has not heard this word, even if he adheres to all the dogmas taught by the Church, has no contact with truth.

—Simone Weil

Art is the lie that enables us to see the truth.

—Pablo Picasso

There is no truer truth obtainable by man than comes of music.

—Robert Browning

Beauty is the index of a larger fact than wisdom.

—Oliver Wendell Holmes,
The Professor at the Breakfast Table

Whatever satisfies the soul is truth.

—Walt Whitman, preface to *Leaves of Grass*

Truth, in every case, is the most reputable victory a man can gain.

—Thomas Paine, *Pennsylvania Packet*

Truth, worship truth!
Nothing in existence is more valuable or noble.
Worship it and reject anything that might corrupt it.

—Naguib Mahfouz, *Mirrors*

Love . . . the truth, by dedicating yourselves carefully to the work of your perfection.

—Pope John Paul II

The pursuit of truth will set you free; even if you never catch up with it.

—Clarence Darrow

The truth which makes men free is for the most part the truth which men prefer not to hear.

—Herbert Sebastian Agar, *A Time for Greatness*

'The pursuit of truth' rightly implies that a gap exists between ourselves and truth. But what's hidden and evasive? Is it we or truth? Maybe it is we who evade truth's quest for us.

—William Sloane Coffin

Face what you think you believe and you will be surprised.

—William Hale White

Truth has rough flavors if we bite it through.

—George Eliot

We don't know a millionth of one percent about anything.

—Thomas A. Edison

I don't mean to suggest that we have the final answers; we are bathing in mystery and confusion on many subjects, and I think that will always be our destiny. **The universe will always be much richer than our ability to understand.**

—Carl Sagan on Cosmos, quoted in "The Cosmos," Jonathan Cott, *Rolling Stone*, December 25, 1980

Everything has been figured out except how to live.

—Jean-Paul Sartre

One must live the way one thinks,
or end up thinking the way one has lived.

–Paul Bourget, French novelist

The ultimate test for us of what a truth means
is the conduct it dictates or inspires.

—William James

[T]o change our realities, we also have to change our myths. As history amply demonstrates, myths and realities go hand in hand.

—Riane Eisler, *Sacred Pleasure*

Somewhere, something incredible is waiting to be known.

—Carl Sagan

5

GUIDING EMOTIONS

A man of genius is unbearable, unless he possesses at least two things besides: gratitude and purity.

Friedrich Nietzsche

What goes on in our minds is important, but so is what goes on in our hearts. Of course, as we saw in some quotations in the previous chapter, and will see in a few more in this one, the divide between the head and the heart is by no means so complete as we often make it out to be. Still, many of us experience some degree of tension between the two, and it's not always easy to resolve it. As Churton Collins said, "Half our mistakes in life arise from feeling where we ought to think, and thinking where we ought to feel." Obviously we can't completely give up one or the other; I suppose we must each try to find our own balance. In this chapter we will explore ideas related to feeling and attitude.

Feelings are transitory; attitude is habitual. We will all experience a range of emotions in our lives, including joy and pain, anger and fear, anxiety and gratitude. The quotations in this chapter are not so much about the feelings themselves as about our response to them. As Katherine Paterson wrote in *Jacob Have I Loved*, "To fear is one thing. To let fear grab you by the tail and swing you around is another." It would seem that there is a power in the human psyche that can function apart from or in opposition to the emotions if necessary—that can encourage some emotions and discourage others. Choosing appropriate ways to deal with emotions is one of the trickiest things we do as humans; fortunately, life seems to give us plenty of opportunities to practice.

Change your thoughts and you change your world.

—Norman Vincent Peale

Sentiment without action is the ruination of the soul.

—Edward Abbey

Beyond all other freedoms our greatest liberty
is our ability to choose our attitude.

—Patricia Ryan Madson, *Improv Wisdom*

One's outlook is a part of his virtue.

—A. Bronson Alcott, *Tablets*

It is something to be able to paint a particular picture, or to carve a statue, or so to make a few objects beautiful; but **it is far more glorious to carve and paint the very atmosphere through which we look**—to affect the quality of the day, that is the highest of the arts.

—Henry David Thoreau

Each of us has the power of transforming the ordinary into the extraordinary—the everyday into the special. To do so is far more rewarding than going the other way around.

—Johnnetta B. Cole, *Dream the Boldest Dreams and Other Lessons of Life*

Life has a bright side and a dark side, for the world of relativity is composed of light and shadows. **If you permit your thoughts to dwell on evil, you yourself will become ugly.** Look only for the good in everything so you absorb the quality of beauty.

—Paramahansa Yogananda

A merry heart doeth good like a medicine.

—Proverbs 17:22

Hate and fear can poison the body as surely as any toxic chemicals.

—Joseph Krimsky, M.D.

Every day give yourself a good mental shampoo.

—Sara Jordan, M.D.

Let's not forget that the little emotions are the great captains of our lives and we obey them without realizing it.

—Vincent Van Gogh

A kind heart is a fountain of gladness,
making everything in its vicinity freshen into smiles.

—Washington Irving

What sunshine is to flowers, smiles are to humanity. They are but trifles, but scattered along life's pathway the good they do is inconceivable.

—Joseph Addison

Those who bring sunshine into the lives of others
cannot keep it from themselves.

—Sir J. M. Barrie

If we really know how to live, what better way to start the day than with a smile? Our smile affirms our awareness and determination to live in peace and joy. **The source of a true smile is an awakened mind.**

—Thich Nhat Hanh, *Peace Is Every Step: The Path of Mindfulness in Everyday Life*

Give me a man who sings at his work.

—Thomas Carlyle

Every day we must dance, if only in our thoughts.

—Rebbe Nachman of Bratslav

You must learn to be still in the midst of activity,
and to be vibrantly alive in repose.

—Indira Gandhi

When my mind is still and alone with the beating of my heart, I find a quiet assurance, an inner peace, in the core of my being. It can face the doubt, the loneliness, the anxiety, can accept these harsh realities and can even grow because of these challenges to my essential being.

—Paul Beattie

Joy is the emotional experience which our kind Father in heaven has attached to the discharge of the most fundamental of all the higher activities—namely, those of inner growth and outer creativeness.

—William Ralph Inge, Dean of St. Paul's Cathedral

Let a joy keep you.
Reach out your hands and take it when it runs by.

—Carl Sandburg

We must live in **joy**.
We must live in **love**.
They are, moreover, **one and the same thing**.

—Moses of Kobrin

Don't worry about the lessons, old boy. . . . Don't get cast down. Sometimes in life, both at school and afterwards, fortune will go against any one, but if he just keeps pegging away and doesn't lose his courage things always take a turn for the better.

—Theodore Roosevelt in a letter to his son Kermit, December 3, 1904

The one sensible thing to do with a disappointment is to put it out of your mind and **think of something cheerfuler.**

—Mark Twain, *Christian Science*

We must accept finite disappointment,
but we must never lose infinite hope.

—Martin Luther King, Jr.

I believe in the sun even when it is not shining.
I believe in love even when not feeling it.
I believe in God even when He is silent.

(Inscription on a cellar well in Cologne, Germany,
where Jews hid from Nazis during World War II)

Hope is a song in a weary throat.

—Pauli Murray, lawyer, minister, and activist

Just as incense refreshes the life of an ember,
so prayer refreshes the hopes of the heart.

—Johann Wolfgang von Goethe, *Wilhelm Meister's Journeyman Years*

I just carry hope in my heart. Hope is not a feeling of certainty, that everything ends well. Hope is just a feeling that life and work have meaning.

—Vaclev Havel

Everything that is done in the world is done by hope.

—Martin Luther

If we have the capacity to endure,
if we have the patience,
things will change.

—César Chávez

Nourish your hopes but do not overlook realities.

—Winston Churchill, in an address to the House of Commons, May 1935

Never face facts; if you do you'll never get up in the morning.

—Marlo Thomas

A good laugh overcomes more difficulties and dissipates
more dark clouds than any other one thing.

—Laura Ingalls Wilder

I love myself when I am laughing.

—Zora Neale Hurston

I can imagine no more comfortable frame of mind for the conduct of
life than a humorous resignation.

—W. Somerset Maugham

No matter what happens,
somebody will find a way to take it too seriously.

—Dave Barry

It takes a clever man to turn cynic,
and a wise man to be clever enough not to.

—attributed to Fannie Hurst, U.S. writer and playwright

Dare to be naïve.

—R. Buckminster Fuller

Woe to the man whose heart has not learned while young to
hope, to love—and to put its trust in life.

—Joseph Conrad

Therefore the True Gentleman spends a lifetime of careful thought, but not
a day in worrying.

—Mencius 4B : 28

I'm determined not to worry. So many people poison every day worrying about the next.

—Jacqueline Kennedy Onassis

You become a worrier by practising worry. You can become free of worry by practising the opposite and stronger habit of faith. With all the strength and perseverance you can command, **start practising faith.**

—Norman Vincent Peale

Never despair, but if you do, work on in despair.

—Edmund Burke

Life begins on the other side of despair.

—Jean-Paul Sartre

Oh! don't the days seem lank and long,
When all goes right and nothing goes wrong?
And isn't life extremely flat
With nothing whatever to grumble at?

—William Schwenck Gilbert, *Princess Ida*

It is easy to find fault, if one has that disposition. There was once a man who, not being able to find any other fault with his coal, complained that there were too many prehistoric toads in it.

—Mark Twain, *Pudd'nhead Wilson's Calendar*

A thankful person is thankful under all circumstances.
A complaining soul complains even if he lives in paradise.

—Baha'u'llah

**Complaining can become a way of boasting
about how much suffering you can endure.**

—Sheldon B. Kopp, *What Took You So Long*

When asked how things are, don't whine and grumble . . . If you answer, 'Lousy,' then God says, 'You call this bad? I'll show you what bad really is!' When asked how things are and, despite hardship or suffering, if you answer, 'Good,' then God says, 'You call this good? I'll show you what good really is!'

—Rebbe Nachman of Bratslav

For the past two weeks you have been reading about the bad break I got. Yet today I consider myself the luckiest man on the face of the earth.

—Lou Gehrig, farewell speech at Yankee Stadium, July 4, 1939, on his retirement because of amyotrophic lateral sclerosis (ALS)

What a wonderful life I've had!
I only wish I'd realized it sooner.

—Colette

Most human beings have an infinite capacity for taking things for granted.

—Aldous Huxley, "Variations on a Philosopher"

Can you see the holiness in those things you take for granted—a paved road or a washing machine? If you concentrate on finding what is good in every situation, you will discover that your life will suddenly be filled with gratitude, a feeling that nurtures the soul.

—Rabbi Harold Kushner

For, after all, put it as we may to ourselves, we are all of us from birth to death guests at a table which we did not spread. The sun, the earth, love, friends, our very breath are parts of the banquet.

—Rebecca Harding Davis

There is a calmness to a life lived in gratitude, a quiet joy.

—Ralph H. Blum

When you clench your fist,
no one can put anything in your hand.

—Alex Haley

Anybody can become angry—that is easy; but to be angry
with the right person,
and to the right degree,
and at the right time,
and for the right purpose,
and in the right way
—that is not within everybody's power and is not easy.

—Aristotle

I have learnt through bitter experience the one supreme lesson to conserve my anger, and as heat conserved is transmuted into energy, even so our anger controlled can be transmuted into a power which can move the world.

—Mahatma Gandhi, *All Men Are Brothers*

Complacency is a far more dangerous attitude than outrage.

—Naomi Littlebear

For who would live so petty and unblest
That dare not tilt at something ere he die!

–John Galsworthy

Even in winter it shall be green in my heart.

—Frédéric Chopin, letter to Tytus Wojciechowski, Warsaw, September 18, 1830

I do not approve of mourning,
I approve only of remembering!

—Noël Coward

Those who do not know how
to weep with their whole heart
don't know how to laugh either.

—Golda Meir

God allows us to experience the low points of life in order to teach us
lessons we could not learn in any other way. The way we learn those lessons
is not to deny the feelings but to find the meanings underlying them.

—Stanley Lindquist

We must embrace pain and burn it
as fuel for our journey.

—Miyazawa Kenji

Learning to accept what was
unthinkable changes you.

—Jacqueline Kennedy Onassis, two years after the assassination of her husband

The only thing for me was to accept everything. Since then—curious as it will no doubt sound to you—I have been happier.

—Oscar Wilde, *De Profundis*

If you surrender to the wind, you can ride it.

—Toni Morrison

The art of life is not controlling what happens to us, but using what happens to us.

—Gloria Steinem, *Revolution from Within*

You walk in grace or you walk in fear. You can't have it both ways.

—Carlos Santana, Carlos Santana website

Only those are fit to live who do not fear to die; and none are fit to die who have shrunk from the joy of life and the duty of life.

—Theodore Roosevelt

Nothing in life is to be feared. It is only to be understood.

—Marie Curie

To defend one's self against fear is simply to insure that one will, one day, be conquered by it; fears must be faced.

—James Baldwin, *The Fire Next Time*

Love, not fear, must be our guide.

—Rosa Parks, *Dear Mrs. Parks: A Dialogue with Today's Youth*

When the heart is flooded with love there is no room in it for fear, for doubt, for hesitation.

—Anne Morrow Lindbergh, *Gift from the Sea*

If you are in harmony with yourself, you may meet a lion without fear, because he respects anyone with self-confidence.

—Nelson Mandela

Courage is the price that Life exacts for granting peace.

—Amelia Earhart

Courage is resistance to fear, mastery of fear, not absence of fear.

—Mark Twain

The greatest test of courage on the earth
is to bear defeat without losing heart.

—R. G. Ingersoll, The Declaration of Independence

The only courage that matters is the kind that gets you
from one moment to the next.

—Mignon McLaughlin

It isn't for the moment you are struck that you need courage, but for
the long uphill climb back to sanity and faith and security.

—Anne Morrow Lindbergh, *Hour of Gold, Hour of Lead: Diaries and Letters of Anne
Morrow Lindbergh*

Security is mostly a superstition. It does not exist in nature, nor do the children of men as a whole experience it. Avoiding danger is no safer in the long run than outright exposure. Life is either a daring adventure, or nothing.

—Helen Keller, *The Open Door*

I say to the young: **Do not stop thinking of life as an adventure.** You have no security unless you can live bravely, excitingly, imaginatively.

—Eleanor Roosevelt

Imagination is the highest kite one can fly.

—Lauren Bacall

I believe that imagination is stronger than knowledge.
That myth is more potent than history.
That dreams are more powerful than facts.
That hope always triumphs over experience.
That laughter is the only cure for grief.
And I believe that love is stronger than death.

—the Storyteller's Creed, from Robert Fulghum's *All I Really Need to Know I Learned in Kindergarten*

6

DREAMS, DESIRES, AND PERSONAL QUESTS

Geniuses are the luckiest of mortals because what they must do is the same as what they most want to do.

W. H. Auden

It's curious in a way that we've come to associate the word "dreams" with wishes, desires, or goals. Although Freud taught that the subconscious mind expresses its repressed desires in symbolic form during sleep, our actual dreams, in the literal sense, are certainly distinct from what we mean when we say that we want our dreams to come true (as anyone who has read C. S. Lewis's *The Voyage of the Dawn Treader* will recall!) It is more likely the seeming insubstantiality of our hopes that causes us to call them "dreams." But just because something is insubstantial doesn't necessarily mean that it has no value.

It's up to you to figure out what the authors of these quotes are thinking of when they use the word "dream." Perhaps it is more straightforward simply to talk about desires or wishes, but the questions of what to do about them are no less thorny. Here you'll also find conflicting views on the question of how—or whether—to pursue the most basic wish, happiness, and of what the consequences might be when we do. For whatever we are in search of, the choices we make in our quest for it may matter more than the dream we started out with.

Within each of us blooms a wellspring
of abundance and opportunity.
For in each of us
rests a deeply personal dream
waiting to be plucked.

—Doris Price

Dreams are the touchstones of our character.

—Henry David Thoreau, *A Week on the Concord and Merrimack Rivers*

We must dare to dream great dreams—
and then we must dare to put them into action.

—Peter MacDonald

Toil, feel, think, hope;
you will be sure to dream enough
before you die, without arranging for it.

—John Sterling

A man who doesn't dream
is like a man who doesn't sweat.
He stores up a lot of poison.

—Truman Capote

The people who think they are happy
should rummage through their dreams.

–Edward Dahlberg

To fit our dreams into our lives, we must first commit to the idea that they
are necessary and important.

—Suzanne Falter-Barns, *Living Your Joy*

**It is those with the boldest dreams
who awaken the best in all of us.**

—Johnnetta B. Cole, *Dream the Boldest Dreams And Other Lessons of Life*

There are people who put their dreams in a little box and say, 'Yes, I've got dreams, of course I've got dreams.' Then they put the box away and bring it out once in awhile to look in it, and yep, they're still there. These are great dreams, but they never even get out of the box. **It takes an uncommon amount of guts to put your dreams on the line**, to hold them up and say, 'How good or how bad am I?' That's where courage comes in.

—Erma Bombeck

Your own words are the bricks and mortar of the dreams you want to realize. Your words are the greatest power you have. The words you choose and their use establish the life you experience.

—Sonia Croquette

One can never consent to creep when one feels an impulse to soar.

—Helen Keller, in a speech at Mt. Airy

I would be the least among men with dreams and the desire to fulfill them, rather than the greatest with no dreams and no desires.

—Kahlil Gibran

Sooner murder an infant in its cradle
than nurse unacted desires.

—William Blake, *The Marriage of Heaven and Hell*

It is much easier to suppress a first desire than to satisfy those that follow.

—François de La Rochefoucauld

You can have anything you want if you want it desperately enough. You must want it with an inner exuberance that erupts through the skin and joins the energy that created the world.

—Sheila Graham

If your wish is strong enough, you may end up actually doing something to make it come true.

—Lloyd Alexander, *The Wizard in the Tree*

My mother said that if you visualize something happening, you can make it happen ... If you are about to run a race, you visualize yourself running the race and crossing the finish line first, and presto! ... The only thing I did not understand was what if everyone visualized himself winning the race?

—Sharon Creech, *Walk Two Moons*

I have only one life, and it is short enough.
Why waste it on things I don't want most?

—Louis D. Brandeis, American jurist

**One half of knowing what you want
is knowing what you must give up before you get it.**

—Sidney Howard

I think people ought to fulfill sacredly their desires.
And this means fulfilling the deepest desire, which is a desire to
live unhampered by things that are extraneous, a desire for pure
relationships and living truth.

—D. H. Lawrence, letter to Catherine Carswell, July 16, 1916

Mans desires are limited by his perceptions; none can desire what he has not perceiv'd.

—William Blake, *There is No Natural Religion*

Nothing is more insidious than the evolution of wishes from mere fancies, and of wants from mere wishes.

—Thomas Hardy

Graceful freedom is having the courage to be satisfied.

—Sam Keen, *To a Dancing God: Notes of a Spiritual Traveler*

In the world there are only two tragedies.
One is not getting what one wants,
and the other is getting it.

—Oscar Wilde, *Lady Windermere's Fan*

Man finds it hard to get what he wants, because he does not want the best; God finds it hard to give, because He would give the best, and man will not take it.

—George MacDonald, "Life," *Unspoken Sermons*, Second Series

It's a funny thing about life;
if you refuse to accept anything but the best,
you very often get it.

—W. Somerset Maugham

I didn't expect anything much and because of that I'm the least bitter woman I know.

—Audrey Hepburn

Knowledge of what is possible is the beginning of happiness.

—George Santayana

The Constitution only guarantees the American people the right to pursue happiness—you have to catch it yourself.

—Benjamin Franklin

Nothing is so difficult but that it may be found out by seeking.

—Terence, *The Self-Tormenter*

Those who want Happiness must stoop to find it; it is a flower that grows in every vale.

—William Blake, "Contemplation"

The secret of happiness is this: Let your interests be as wide as possible, and let your reactions to the things and persons that interest you be as far as possible friendly rather than hostile.

—Bertrand Russell

A mind always employed is always happy.
This is the true secret, the grand recipe for felicity.

—Thomas Jefferson, to Martha Jefferson, May 21, 1787

Creativity is harnessing universality and making it flow through your eyes . . . The greatest happiness in life is to be truly and consistently creative.

—Peter Koestenbaum

Learn to value yourself, which means:
to fight for your happiness.

—Ayn Rand

True happiness is of a retired nature, and an enemy to pomp and noise; it arises, in the first place, from the enjoyment of one's self; and, in the next, from the friendship and conversation of a few select companions.

—Joseph Addison, *The Spectator*

Everything in excess!
To enjoy the flavor of life, take big bites.
Moderation is for monks.

—excerpt from the notebooks of Lazarus Long, from Robert A. Heinlein's *Time Enough for Love*

Don't smoke too much, drink too much, eat too much, or work too much.
We're all on the road to the grave,
but there's no need to be in the passing lane.

—Robert Orben

Life itself is the proper binge.

—Julia Child

**One reason I don't drink is that
I want to know when I'm having a good time.**

—Lady Nancy Astor

Pleasure is the object, duty and the goal of all rational creatures.

—Voltaire

I can think of nothing less pleasurable
than a life devoted to pleasure.

—John D. Rockefeller

It's pretty hard to tell what does bring happiness;
poverty and wealth have both failed.

—Frank McKinney Hubbard

Ask yourself whether you are happy, and you cease to be so.

—John Stuart Mill, *Autobiography*

The best way to attain happiness is not to seek it.

—Claude G. Montefiore,
Liberal Judaism

**If only we'd stop trying to be happy,
we could have a pretty good time.**

—Edith Wharton

The bird of paradise alights only on the hand that does not grasp.

—John Berry

He who binds to himself a joy,
Doth the winged life destroy;
But he who kisses the joy as it flies,
Lives in Eternity's sunrise.

–William Blake

Happiness makes up in height for what it lacks in length.

–Robert Frost

It is our quality that matters:
take care of that, and our happiness will take care of itself.

—George Bernard Shaw, *The Intelligent Woman's Guide to Socialism, Capitalism, Sovietism & Fascism*

Simply seek happiness and you are not likely to find it. **Seek to create and love** without regard to your happiness and you are likely to be happy much of the time.

—M. Scott Peck

True happiness comes from a sense of peace and contentment, which in turn must be achieved through the cultivation of altruism, of love and compassion, and elimination of ignorance, selfishness, and greed.

—Tenzin Gyatso, the Fourteenth Dalai Lama, Nobel Acceptance Speech, December10, 1989

As I grow older I realize that **the only pleasure I have in anything is to share it with someone else.**

—Eleanor Roosevelt, "What I Hope to Leave Behind," in *Pictorial Review* 34, April 1933

Next to enjoying happiness ourselves,
is the consciousness of having bestowed it on others.

—Sir Walter Scott, *The Black Dwarf*

The best way to secure future happiness is to be as happy as is rightfully possible to-day.

—Charles W. Eliot, *The Happy Life*

The end is nothing, the road is all.

—Willa Cather

He came to a wall so high he feared his tiny horse could not carry him over; but the fairy king said to him, 'Throw your heart over the wall, then follow it!' So [the mortal] rode fearlessly at the wall, with his heart already bravely past it, and went safely over.

—Laura Ingalls Wilder

Most people don't lead their own lives— they accept their lives.

—John Kotter

Two questions you had better ask yourself—and make sure you get them in the right order: Where am I going? Who am I going with?

—Johnnetta B. Cole, *Dream the Boldest Dreams and Other Lessons of Life*

Don't go where the path leads.
Go where there is no path and leave a trail.

—Ralph Waldo Emerson

It is the privilege and proper condition of a human being, arrived at the maturity of his faculties, to use and interpret experience in his own way.

—John Stuart Mill, *On Liberty*

Follow the truth of the way.
Reflect upon it.
Make it your own.
Live it.
It will always sustain you.

— Siddhartha Gautama, the Buddha,
from the Dhammapada, translated by Thomas Byrom

Life is like riding a bicycle; in order to keep your balance,
you must keep moving.

—Albert Einstein to his son

I know what I am fleeing from, but not what I am in search of.

—Michel de Montaigne

All human beings should try to learn before they die what they are
running from, and to, and why.

—James Thurber

Know from whence you came.
If you know whence you came,
there is really no limit to where you can go.

—James Baldwin, *The Fire Next Time*

Have patience with everything unresolved in your heart
and try to love the questions themselves.

—Rainer Maria Rilke, *Letters to a Young Poet*

Every step of the journey is the journey.

—Zen saying

When real truth stamps the mind, the path becomes self-evident. If the mind is not true, then even if you attend lectures every day and discuss the path constantly, this just provides topics of conversation and is ultimately of no benefit on the path.

—Hui-k'ung, Zen master

The road to the next duty is the only straight one.

—George MacDonald, *The Princess and Curdie*

We have not even to risk the adventure alone, for the heroes of all time have gone before us—the labyrinth is thoroughly known. We have only to follow the thread of the hero path.

—Joseph Campbell

A man travels the world in search of what he needs and returns home to find it.

—George Moore, *The Brook Kerith*

We plan our lives according to a dream that came to us in our childhood, and we find that life alters our plans. And yet, at the end, from a rare height, we also see that our dream was our fate.

—Ben Okri, Nigerian author

Destiny is a mysterious thing, sometimes enfolding a miracle in a leaky basket of catastrophe.

—Francisco Goldman

Actions are the seeds of fate. **Deeds grow into destiny.**

—Harry S. Truman

Destiny is not a matter of chance, it is a matter of choice;
it is not a thing to be waited for, it is a thing to be achieved.

—William Jennings Bryan

We choose our joys and our sorrows long before we experience
them.

—Kahlil Gibran, *Sand and Foam*

Every beginning is a consequence—every beginning ends some thing.

—Paul Valéry

Before a seed germinates it must first decay.

—Ali A. Mazrui, *The Africans: A Triple Heritage*

Everything you now do is something you have chosen to do.

—John C. Maxwell, *Today Matters*

We do not choose to be born. We do not choose our parents. We do not choose our historical epoch, the country of our birth, or the immediate circumstances of our upbringing . . . But **within this realm of choicelessness, we do choose how we live.**

—Joseph Epstein

Every day, either you live by priorities or you live by pressures. There is no other option. Either you decide what is important in your life, or you let other people decide what is important in your life.

—Rick Warren, *God's Answers to Life's Difficult Questions*

As one grew older, he said, one learned that with
enough care almost anything would keep.
It was only a matter of choosing what to take care of.

—Barry López, *Winter Count*

One cannot collect all the beautiful shells on the beach. One can collect
only a few, and they are more beautiful if they are few.

—Anne Morrow Lindbergh

Warning: Be careful what you spend your day touching because it
will shape your mind, your body, and your heart.

—Sam Keen, preface to the 1990 edition of *To a Dancing God: Notes of a Spiritual Traveller*

Riches have made more covetous men than
covetousness hath made rich men.

—Thomas Fuller

We can tell our values by looking at our checkbook stubs.

—Gloria Steinem

It is not true that love makes all things easy:
it makes us choose what is difficult.

—George Eliot, *Felix Holt*

And if you will here stop and ask yourself why you are not as pious as the primitive Christians were, your own heart will tell you that it is neither through ignorance nor inability, but purely because you never thoroughly intended it.

—William Law, *A Serious Call to a Devout and Holy Life*

People wish to learn to swim and at the same time to keep one foot on the ground.

—Marcel Proust

Morality may consist solely in the courage of making a choice.

—Léon Blum, French socialist

Decision is a sharp knife that cuts clean and straight. Indecision is a dull one that hacks and tears and leaves ragged edges behind.

—Jan McKeithen

Just because you have a choice, it doesn't mean that any of them has to be right.

—Norton Juster, *The Phantom Tollbooth*

Thus, and not otherwise, the world was made. Either something or nothing must depend on individual choices. And if something, who could set bounds to it? **A stone may determine the course of a river.**

—C. S. Lewis, *Perelandra*

[We] go lightheartedly on our way never thinking that **by a careless word or two we may have altered the whole course of human lives**, for some persons will take [our] advice and use it.

—Laura Ingalls Wilder

Seldom do we do just one thing when we take action.

—W. Edward Harris

Those who profess to favor freedom, yet deprecate agitation, are men who want crops without plowing the ground; they want rain without thunder and lightning; they want the ocean without the awful roar of its many waters.

—Frederick Douglass

Too many times for comfort I have expected to reap good when I know I have sown evil . . . Now . . . I try to plant peace if I do not want discord; to plant loyalty and honesty if I want to avoid betrayal and lies.

—Maya Angelou, *Wouldn't Take Nothing for My Journey Now*

You can't reach good ends through evil means, because the means represent the seed and the end represents the tree.

—Martin Luther King, Jr.

You can't hold a man down without staying down with him.

—Booker T. Washington

It is not what is done to us, but what is made of us, that wrongs us. No man can be really injured but by what modifies himself.

—Olive Schreiner, *Story of an African Farm*

I can be changed by what happens to me, but I refuse to be reduced by it.

—Maya Angelou

So it is, life is actually made up of our choices. We are the sum total of them, and if we hold to an attitude of love and thanksgiving for all the good things within our grasp we may have what all ambitious people long for—success.

—Delma Neeley

7

SUCCESS AND GREATNESS

True genius lies not in doing extraordinary things but in doing ordinary things extraordinarily well.

Maj. Gen. Louis H. Wilson

Like happiness, success is something that most people would say they want but that may take different forms for different people. You may already have some notions, either your own or those of society, about what would constitute success for you. In this chapter, we will see a number of different ways of defining it from people who achieved starkly different kinds of success in their lives. There's also advice about how to achieve success and some sobering thoughts about the possibility of failure.

Perhaps success is easiest to define when it's limited to a specific goal we're trying to reach, which is usually another way of saying that we've got a problem we're trying to solve. I've included a few quotations about problems and problem-solving here.

Despite the overwhelming size and nature of the obstacles that life presents, some people have been able to overcome them to a degree that makes them stand out as someone special—someone extraordinary, someone great. We may call them a genius or even a hero. How are these wonderful people different from the rest of us? Or, perhaps we should ask: how different are they? Can all of us aspire to greatness? Do we want to? In the last part of this chapter, I've collected a number of quotes relating to the idea of the great individual. Here, again, the question of what greatness means is an open one, one which you'll have to think about for yourself as you read each quotation.

Success is not the key to happiness. Happiness is the key to success.

—Albert Schweitzer, philosopher, physician, musician, Nobel laureate

Success can corrupt; usefulness can only exalt.

—Dimitri Mitropolous

There are no secrets to success; don't waste time looking for them. Success is the result of perfection, hard work, learning from failure, loyalty to those for whom you work, and persistence.

—Colin Powell

Nothing works unless you do.

—Maya Angelou

Rise early. Work late. Strike oil.

—J. Paul Getty

Chance favors the prepared mind.

—Louis Pasteur

An aim in life is the only fortune worth finding.

—Robert Louis Stevenson

Winning the prize wasn't half as exciting as doing the work itself.

—Maria Goeppert Mayer, recipient of 1963 Nobel Prize in physics

I believe most men will make good if they find the work they are happy in doing.

—Harvey Firestone

Success cannot be guaranteed. There are no safe battles.

—Winston Churchill

When you are in any contest, you should work as if there were
to the very last minute—a chance to lose it.
This is battle, this is politics, this is anything.

—Dwight D. Eisenhower

The difference between an unsuccessful person and others is not a lack of strength, not a lack of knowledge, but rather a lack of will.

—Vince Lombardi

If I am asked whether the American people will pull themselves out of this depression, I answer, 'They will if they want to.'

—Franklin Delano Roosevelt, *Fireside Chat*

Every try will not succeed. If you live, your business is trying.

—John Oliver Killens

Everything looks impossible for the people who never try anything.

—Jean-Louis Etienne

I am not discouraged, because every wrong attempt discarded is another step forward.

—Thomas A. Edison

Those who have stood high on Fortune's wheel, must abide by the consequences of its revolutions.

—Sir Walter Scott, *Peveril of the Peak*

Half of the failures in life come from pulling one's horse when he is leaping.

—Thomas Hood

No man is a failure who is enjoying life.

—William Feather

You fail only when you let death creep in and take over a part of your life that should be alive.

—Bob Dylan

The only failure a man ought to fear is failure in cleaving to the purpose he sees to be best. As to just the amount of result he may see from his particular work—that's a tremendous uncertainty: the universe has not been arranged for the gratification of his feelings.

—George Eliot, *Felix Holt*

Good losers get into the habit of losing.

—George Allen

Win as if you were used to it,
lose as if you enjoyed it for a change.

—Eric Mark Golnik

I don't know why we are in such a hurry to get up when we fall down. You might think we would lie there and rest awhile.

—Max Eastman

The sheer rebelliousness in giving ourselves permission to fail frees a childlike awareness and clarity . . .
**When we give ourselves permission to fail,
we at the same time give ourselves permission to excel.**

—Eloise Ristad

Go on failing. Go on. Only next time, try to fail better.

—Samuel Beckett, to an actor who said, "I'm failing"

He who limps is still walking.

—Stanislaw J. Lec

There is no wealth but life.

—John Ruskin

Don't judge each day by the harvest you reap,
but by the seeds you plant.

—Robert Louis Stevenson

At the moment of death we will not be judged according to the number of good deeds we have done or by the diplomas we have received in our lifetime. We will be judged according to the love we have put into our work.

—Mother Teresa

Judge a tree from its fruit, not from the leaves.

—Euripides

Success is not always an accomplishment. It can be a state of mind. The quiet dignity of a home, the relationship of the individuals in the home. The continuing expression of an inquiring mind can mean more in terms of success than all the surface symbols of status.

—Lady Bird Johnson

Success is liking yourself, liking what you do, and liking how you do it.

—Maya Angelou

We cannot seek achievement for ourselves and forget about progress and prosperity for our community . . . Our ambitions must be broad enough to include the aspirations and needs of others, for their sakes and for our own.

—César Chávez

Try not to become a man of success
but rather try to become a man of value.

—Albert Einstein

To leave the world richer—that is the ultimate success.

—Eleanor Roosevelt

Each success only buys an admission ticket to a more difficult problem.

—Henry A. Kissinger, *Wilson Library Bulletin*

The way we see the problem is the problem.

—Stephen Covey, *The 7 Habits of Highly Effective People*

The answers are always inside the problem, not outside.

—Marshall McLuhan

If we want to solve a problem that we have never solved before, we must leave the door to the unknown ajar.

—Richard P. Feynman, *What Do You Care What Other People Think?*

The sovereign remedy for an ill effect
Is the extinction of its evil cause.

—Thomas Hardy

The first requisite of intelligent tinkering is to save all the pieces.

—Aldo Leopold

Being able to predict which problems you are not likely to solve is good for your peace of mind.

—Edward Hodnett, *The Art of Problem Solving*

Troubles are tools by which God fashions us for better things.

—Henry Ward Beecher

The ultimate way is without difficulty; those who seek it make their own hardship. **The true mind is originally pure**; those who exercise it make their own defilement.

—Hui-k'ung, Zen master

Understanding love is one of the hardest things in the world.

—Fred Rogers

Life becomes harder for us
when we live for others,
but it also becomes richer and happier.

—Albert Schweitzer

Not everything that is more difficult is more meritorious.

—St. Thomas Aquinas

If it weren't for the rocks in its bed,
the stream would have no song.

—Carl Perkins

Out of every crisis, every tribulation, every disaster,
mankind rises with some share of greater knowledge,
of higher decency, of purer purpose.

—Franklin Delano Roosevelt, speech at Democratic Convention
in Chicago, July 2, 1932, accepting the nomination for president

We shall draw from the heart of suffering itself the means of
inspiration and survival.

—Winston Churchill

I do not believe that sheer suffering teaches. If suffering alone taught, all the world would be wise, since everyone suffers. To suffering must be added mourning, understanding, patience, love, openness, and the willingness to remain vulnerable.

—Anne Morrow Lindbergh

Where there is sorrow there is holy ground. Some day you will realize what this means. You will know nothing of life till you do.

—Oscar Wilde, *De Profundis*

All sorrows can be borne, if you put them into a story.

—Isak Dinesen

God, pitying the toils which our race is born to undergo, gave us the gift of song.

—Plato

There must be quite a few things a hot bath won't cure, but I don't know many of them.

—Sylvia Plath

Nothing splendid has ever been achieved except by those who dared believe that something inside them was superior to circumstance.

—Bruce Barton

Little minds are tamed and subdued by misfortune; but great minds rise above it.

—Washington Irving

The ordinary man is involved in action,
the hero acts. An immense difference.

—Henry Miller, *The Books in My Life*

Enlightenment is just another word
for feeling comfortable with being
a completely ordinary person.

—Veronique Vienne, *The Art of Doing Nothing*

Deep within man dwell those slumbering powers;
powers that would astonish him, that he
never dreamed of possessing; forces that would
revolutionize his life if aroused
and put into action.

—Orison Swett Marden

Everyone has talent. What is rare is the courage
to follow the talent to the dark place where it leads.

—Erica Jong, "The Artist as Housewife: The Housewife as Artist," *The First Ms. Reader*

When you are inspired by some great
purpose, some extraordinary project,
all your thoughts break their bonds;
Your mind transcends limitations,
your consciousness expands in every direction,
and you find yourself in a new, great
and wonderful world.
Dormant forces, faculties and talents
become alive, and you discover yourself
to be a greater person by far
than you ever dreamed
yourself to be.

—Patanjali, *Yoga Sutras*

After months of inward darkness, I suddenly had the everlasting conviction that any human being, even though practically devoid of natural faculties, can penetrate to the kingdom of truth reserved for genius, if only he longs for truth and perpetually concentrates all his attention upon its attainment.

—Simone Weil

What we call talent is not so much a gift as an opportunity.

—Roger Peters, *Practical Intelligence*

If we all did the things we are capable of doing, we would literally astound ourselves.

—Thomas A. Edison

Recall that whatever lofty things you might accomplish today, you will do them only because you first ate something that grew out of dirt.

—Barbara Kingsolver

It is impossible to get the measure of what an individual can accomplish unless the responsibility is given him.

—Alfred P. Sloan, Jr.

A hero is someone who understands the responsibility that comes with his freedom.

—Bob Dylan

Kill reverence and you've killed the hero in man.

—Ayn Rand, *The Fountainhead*

Self-trust is the essence of heroism.

—Ralph Waldo Emerson, "Heroism"

**To have doubted one's own first principles
is the mark of a civilized man.**

—Oliver Wendell Holmes, Jr.

Who says I am not under the special protection of God?

—Adolf Hitler

Men of the most exalted genius and active minds are generally most perfect slaves to the love of fame. . . . The greatest men have been the most envious, malicious, and revengeful.

—from the diary of John Adams, February 19, 1756

I believe that the first test of a truly great man is his humility . . . Really great men have a curious feeling that the greatness is not in them, but through them. And they see something divine in every other man and are endlessly, foolishly, incredibly merciful.

—John Ruskin, *Of Modern Landscape*

Keep away from people who
try to belittle your ambitions.
Small people always do that,
but the really great make you feel that you,
too, can become great.

—Mark Twain

I have not the shadow of a doubt that any man or woman can achieve
what I have, if he or she would make the same effort and cultivate the
same hope and faith.

—Mahatma Gandhi, *All Men Are Brothers*

Holiness is not the luxury of a few. It is everyone's duty:
yours and mine.

—Mother Teresa

The way of the world is to praise dead saints and to persecute live ones.

—Nathaniel Howe

The saints are the sinners who keep on trying.

—Robert Louis Stevenson

I have never been especially impressed by the heroics of people convinced that they are about to change the world, I am more awed by those who struggle to make one small difference after another.

—Ellen Goodman

Yet such is oft the course of deeds that move the wheels of the world: small hands do them because they must, while the eyes of the great are elsewhere.

—J. R. R. Tolkien, *The Lord of the Rings*

Love, when it is genuine, is all-embracing, stable and lasting, an irresistible spur to all forms of heroism.

—Pope Paul VI, *Sacerdotalis Caelibatus*

The truest and noblest acts of heroism
are fought unaided in the empty
terror-laden chambers of our hearts.

—Perry A. White, *Reflections*

What have creatures like us to do with heroism who are not yet barely honest?

—George MacDonald, "Life," *Unspoken Sermons*, Second Series

One must think like a hero to behave like a merely decent human being.

—May Sarton

Heroism isn't a conscious thought.
It comes from caring about the people you're with.

—Colin Powell

There are men and women chosen to bring happiness into the
hearts of people—those are the real heroes.

—Nelson Mandela

I would never deny that my parents played an absolutely heroic role in the anti-apartheid struggle. But they were also human beings. And if we cannot allow our heroes to be human beings, we're in serious trouble.

—Gillian Slovo, daughter of South African anti-apartheid activists Joe Slovo and Ruth First, 'Daughter of the Struggle,' *Salon,* June 1997

It's too bad I'm not as wonderful a person as people say I am, because the world could use a few people like that.

—Alan Alda

The world has been waiting for our transformation because it, too, wants transformation. When we are transformed, the world is transformed, because we and the world are one.

—Deepak Chopra, *Power, Freedom, and Grace: Living from the Source of Lasting Happiness*

There are two great beginnings in the life of every man who has left his mark upon history. There is the day when he is born into the world; and there is the day when he discovers why he was born into the world.

—William Barclay, Scottish theologian

This is the true joy in life, the being used for a purpose recognized by yourself as a mighty one; . . . the being a force of Nature, instead of a feverish, selfish little clod of ailments and grievances complaining that the world will not devote itself to making you happy.

—George Bernard Shaw, *Epistle Dedicatory to Man and Superman*

When we are really honest with ourselves we must admit that our lives are all that really belong to us. So, it how we use our lives that determines what kind of men we are. **It is my deepest belief that only by giving our lives do we find life.**

—César Chávez

Just as he who gives his life to serve a great idea is admirable, he who avails himself of a great idea to serve his personal hopes of glory and power is abominable, even if he too risks his life. To give one's life is a right only when one gives it unselfishly.

—José Martí

We give our lives, even an hour at a time, for what we believe, what we value, and whom we love.

—Bruce C. Hafen

8

TIME

Genius seems to consist in the power of applying the originality of youth to the experience of maturity.

Michael Polanyi, *The Study of Man*

We've seen a lot of ways in which life can change. But what is life, in the final analysis, but time? If anything about our lives changes, it will very likely be due at least in part to the way we use, respond to, imagine, or place ourselves in time.

We tend to imagine time in different ways, depending on what we're talking about. When we're talking about our everyday lives, we tend to focus on how much of it we have, or don't have; in other words, we imagine time as a possession or a resource, like money or raw material. But unlike physical resources, time can't be stored up in a vault. We have to practice our thriftiness in time while it flows past us—or perhaps carries us along with it.

The other main way of imagining time is to see not that we have it, but that it contains us—that it is the medium or environment of our lives, like a place. And from that particular place we call the present, we may imagine ourselves looking either forward or backward. The wisdom or folly of doing so is another of the topics raised in this chapter. We interpret the present based on what we know, or think we know, about the past and the future, whether we are setting it against the background of history or of a whole life with its different stages. These voices from the past and from other people's experience of various life stages may help to round out our perspectives of our own time on this earth.

Dost thou love life?
Then do not squander time;
for that's the stuff life is made of.

—Benjamin Franklin, *Poor Richard's Almanack*

Hold every moment sacred. Give each clarity and meaning, each the weight of thine awareness, each its true and due fulfillment.

—Thomas Mann

Why should we need extra time in which to enjoy ourselves? If we expect to enjoy our life, we will have to **learn to be joyful** in all of it, not just at stated intervals when we can get time or when we have nothing else to do.

—Laura Ingalls Wilder

The average man, who does not know what to do with his life, wants another one which will last forever.

—Anatole France, *The Revolt of the Angels*

Life is so rarely lived at its fullest stretch
because so few are able to function
at the same time as if they were going
to live forever and as if they might die tomorrow.

—Sydney J. Harris, *Pieces of Eight*

How many times have you noticed
that **it's the little quiet moments**
in the midst of life that seem to give
the rest extra-special meaning?

—Fred Rogers

As if you could kill time,
without injuring eternity.

—Henry David Thoreau

The days come and go like muffled and veiled figures
sent from a distant friendly party, but they say nothing,
and if we do not use the gifts they bring,
they carry them as silently away.

—Ralph Waldo Emerson, "Days"

Tomorrow comes to us at midnight very clean. It's perfect when it arrives, and it pushes itself in our hands and hopes we've learnt something from yesterday.

—John Wayne

Most people don't know when the best part of the day is: it's the early morning.

—Harry S. Truman

Don't say you don't have enough time. You have exactly the same number of hours per day that were given to Helen Keller, Pasteur, Michaelangelo, Mother Teresa, Leonardo da Vinci, Thomas Jefferson, and Albert Einstein.

—H. Jackson Brown, Jr.

When one has much to put in them,
a day has a hundred pockets.

—Friedrich Nietzsche

Time is the most valuable coin in your life. You and you alone will determine how that coin will be spent. Be careful that you do not let other people spend it for you.

—Carl Sandburg

Procrastination is the thief of time.

—Edward Young

What may be done at any time will be done at no time.

—Scottish proverb

The misfortune is, that partly from the pressing necessity of some instant things, and partly from the impatience of our own tempers, **we are frequently in such a hurry** to make out the meaning of every thing as fast as it happens, that we thereby never truly understand it.

—Thomas Paine, *The American Crisis*

That forethought only is right which has to determine duty, and pass into action. To the foundation of yesterday's work well done, the work of the morrow will be sure to fit.

—George MacDonald, "The Cause of Spiritual Stupidity," *Unspoken Sermons*, Second Series

Why should we live with such hurry and waste of life?
We are determined to be starved before we are hungry.

—Henry David Thoreau, *Walden*

No two things differ more than hurry and dispatch.
Hurry is the mark of a weak mind, dispatch of a strong one.

—Charles Caleb Colton, *Lacon*

There are some good things today about walking.
Not many, but some. Walking takes longer,
for example, than any other known form
of locomotion except crawling.
Thus it stretches time and prolongs life.
Life is already too short to waste on speed.

—Edward Abbey, "Walking"

The trouble with life in the fast lane is that you
get to the other end in an awful hurry.

—John Jensen, Danish soccer star

Defer no time, delays have dangerous ends.

—William Shakespeare, *Henry VI, Part 1*

Had I known life to ebb so swiftly I would have given a tremendous importance to time, giving every heartbeat to the bettering of my understanding of life and consequently of myself.

—Anita Vélez-Mitchell

I don't want to get to the end of my life and find that I lived just the length of it. **I want to have lived the width of it as well.**

—Diane Ackerman

It takes the whole of life to learn how to live, and—
what will perhaps make you wonder more—
it takes the whole of life to learn how to die.

—Seneca, *De brevitate vitae*

Death is terrifying because it is so ordinary.
It happens all the time.

—Susan Cheever

Fear not that your life shall come to an end,
but rather that it shall never have a beginning.

— Cardinal John Henry Newman

Men do not care how nobly they live, but only
how long, although it is within the reach
of every man to live nobly, but within
no man's power to live long.

—Seneca, *Epistulae morales*

Wish not so much to live long as to live well.

—Benjamin Franklin, *Poor Richard's Almanack*

What a melancholy world this would be without children,
and what an inhuman world without the aged.

—Samuel Taylor Coleridge

No child is born a criminal: no child is born an angel: he's just born.

—Sir Sydney Smith, New Zealand-born British forensic scientist and writer,
English politician

The first joy of a child is the knowledge that it is loved.

—Don Bosco

Our lives may be determined less by our childhood than by the way we have learned to imagine our childhoods.

—James Hillman, *The Soul's Code*

I do not believe in a child world . . . I believe the child should be taught from the very first that the whole world is his world, that adult and child share one world, that **all generations are needed.**

—Pearl S. Buck

The distinction between children and adults,
while probably useful for some purposes,
is at bottom a specious one, I feel.
There are only individual egos,
crazy for love.

—Don Barthelme

There is always one moment in childhood when the door opens
and lets the future in.

—Deepak K. Chopra

If you carry your childhood with you, you never become older.

—Tom Stoppard

Perhaps I may record here my protest against the efforts . . . to shield children and young people from all that has to do with death and sorrow, to give them a good time at all hazards . . . Young people themselves often resent this attitude on the part of their elders; they feel set aside and belittled as if they were denied the common human experiences.

—Jane Addams, *Twenty Years at Hull House*

No child is born with a really cold heart,
and it is only in proportion as we lose that youthful
heart that we lose the inner warmth in ourselves.

—Lin Yutang

Too many people grow up. That's the real trouble with the world,
too many people grow up. They forget. They don't remember what
it's like to be twelve years old. They patronize, they treat children as
inferiors.

—Walt Disney

You grow up the day you have your first real laugh at yourself.

—Ethel Barrymore

We have not passed that subtle line between childhood and adulthood until . . . we have stopped saying 'It got lost,' and say 'I lost it.'

—Sydney J. Harris

Youth is not a time of life—it is a state of mind. It is a temper of the will; a quality of the imagination; a vigor of the emotions; it is a freshness of the deep springs of life. Youth means a temperamental predominance of courage over timidity, of the appetite for adventure over a life of ease . . . Nobody grows old by merely living a number of years; **people grow old by deserting their ideals.**

—Samuel Ullman, "Youth"

The great thing about getting older
is that you don't lose all the other ages you've been.

—Madeleine L'Engle

311

How foolish to think that one can ever slam the door in the face of age.
Much wiser to be polite and gracious and ask him to lunch in advance.

—Noël Coward, diary, June 3, 1956

There is more felicity on the far side of baldness
than young men can possibly imagine.

—Logan Pearsall Smith

We grow neither better nor worse as we get old,
but more like ourselves.

—Mary Lamberton Becker

Anyone who keeps the ability to see beauty never grows old.

—Franz Kafka

You and I remained like children our entire lives, and that's what makes life so wonderful. We retain that childlike awe.

—Albert Einstein, quoted by biographer Walter Isaacson
in an NPR interview, April 9, 2007

The paradox is that you cannot remain young until you have matured.

—Sydney J. Harris, *Pieces of Eight*

I am as young as the most beautiful wish in my heart—and as old as all the unfulfilled longings in my life . . .

—Elderly Kung Bushman's answer to how old he was

To know how to grow old is the master work of wisdom, and one of the most difficult chapters in the great art of living.

—Henri-Frederic Amiel

For the unlearned, old age is winter; for the learned, it is the season of harvest.

—Yiddish maxim

The longer I live the more beautiful life becomes.

—Frank Lloyd Wright

The years seem to rush by now, and I think of death as a fast approaching end of a journey—double and treble reasons for loving as well as working while it is day.

—George Eliot, *Life and Letters*

Death is psychologically as important as birth. . . .
Shrinking away from it is something unhealthy
and abnormal which robs the second half of life of its purpose.

—Carl Gustav Jung, quoted in *Time*, obituary, June 16, 1961

We die daily. Happy those who daily come to life as well.

—George MacDonald, *Wilfred Cumbermede*

Believe me, a wise man never says, 'I shall live'; to live tomorrow is too late: live today.

—Marcus Valerius Martialis (Martial), *Epigrammata*, I., 15, 11

Let us not bankrupt our todays by paying interest on the regrets of yesterday and by borrowing in advance the troubles of tomorrow.

—Ralph W. Sockman

We should be blessed if we lived in the present always, and took advantage of every accident that befell us . . . and did not spend our time in atoning for the neglect of past opportunities, which we call doing our duty.

—Henry David Thoreau, *Walden*

When you say 'I would die for you' to those you love, the truth of those words may be not that you give your physical life but that you are willing to die to the past and **be born again in the present where you can live fully and freely**—where you can give us the love we need.

—bell hooks, in her dedication in *Bone Black: Memories of Girlhood*

You have to know the past to understand the present.

—Carl Sagan

Life can only be understood backwards; but it must be lived forwards.

—Sören Kierkegaard

I don't look back and say, 'Oh, gee.'
There's no use living that way.
Do the best you can and look forward.

—Sandra Day O'Connor, in *Newsweek* February 12, 2007

To be happy, drop the words 'if only' and substitute instead the words 'next time.'

—Smiley Blanton

Yesterday I loved, today I suffer, tomorrow I shall die. Nonetheless I still think with pleasure, today and tomorrow, of yesterday.

—Gotthold Ephraim Lessing, 'Song Taken from the Spanish'

Squeeze the past like a sponge,
smell the present like a rose,
and
send a kiss to the future.

—Arabic proverb

[God] made the world round so we would not be able to see too far down the road.

—Isak Dinesen

Every man is his own ancestor, and every man is his own heir.
He devises his own future, and he inherits his own past.

—Fredrick Henry Hedge

We are going to have to be rather clever people if we are going to escape from our own cleverness in the past.

—Sir Mark Oliphant

Politics offers yesterday's answers to today's problems.

—Marshall McLuhan

Human nature will not change. In any future great national trial, compared with the men of this, we shall have as weak and as strong, as silly and as wise, as bad and as good. Let us therefore study the incidents of this, as philosophy to learn wisdom from, and none of them as wrongs to be revenged.

—Abraham Lincoln

There is nothing permanent except change.

—Heraclitus

Do not seek to follow in the footsteps of the men of old;
seek what they sought.

—Matsuo Basho, "The Rustic Gate"

So often I heard people paying blind obeisance to change—as though it had some virtue of its own. Change or we will die. Change or we will stagnate. Evergreens don't stagnate.

—Judith Rossner

'Are we never to get out of the old groove?'
'Not if the groove is good.'

—Anthony Trollope, *Phineas Finn*, LXV

Chains of habit are too light to be felt
until they are too heavy to be broken.

—Warren Buffett

If you disable change, if you effectively stop time, if you prevent
the possibility of the alteration of an individual's circumstances—
and that must include at least the possibility that they alter for the
worse—then you don't have life after death; you just have death.

—Iain M. Banks, *Look to Windward*

Upon the growing accuracy with which we
are able to judge our limitations and our
potentialities, as human beings and in
particular as human societies, will depend
the survival of our civilization,
which we now have the means to destroy.

—Margaret Mead

Those who cannot remember the past
are condemned to repeat it.

—George Santayana

We are at an epochal, transitional moment
in the history of life on Earth.
There is no other time as risky,
but no other time as promising
for the future of life on our planet.

—Carl Sagan, *Cosmic Connection*

I've got news for Mr. Santayana:
we're doomed to repeat the past
no matter what.
That's what it is to be alive.

—Kurt Vonnegut, Jr., *Bluebeard*

Civilization is a race between education and catastrophe.

—H. G. Wells

[I am] a man whose invincible belief is that Science and Peace will triumph over Ignorance and War, that nations will unite, not to destroy, but to build, and that the future will belong to those who will have done most for suffering humanity.

—Louis Pasteur in a speech at his Golden Jubilee, December 27, 1892

The end of the human race will be that it will eventually
die of civilization.

—Ralph Waldo Emerson

Maybe civilization is coming to an end, but it still exists, and meanwhile we
have our choice: We can either rain more blows on it, or try to redeem it.

—Saul Bellow

The last struggle for our rights,
the battle for our civilization,
is entirely with ourselves.

—William Wells Brown

Apocalypse is the eye of a needle,
through which we pass into a different world.

—George Zebrowski, *Macrolife*

I got . . . the idea that what you were supposed to do was be plenty morbid and predict the end of civilization many times, but civilization has ended so many times during my brief term on earth that I got a little bored with the theme.

—Howard Nemerov

Our ignorance of history makes us libel our own times.
People have always been like this.

—Gustave Flaubert

We are called to be the architects of the future,
not its victims.

—R. Buckminster Fuller

Those old stories of visions and dreams guiding men have their truth: we are saved by making the future present to ourselves.

—George Eliot, *Felix Holt*

It is a mistake to look too far ahead. Only one link in the chain of destiny can be handled at a time.

—Winston Churchill, in a speech in the House after the Yalta Conference, 1945

The ultimate test of a moral society is the kind of world it leaves to its children.

—Rev. Dietrich Bonhoeffer

Real generosity towards the future lies in giving all to the present.

—Albert Camus

Let us be glad to live in these times of ours, and let us courageously commit ourselves to the design which Providence is mysteriously accomplishing.

—Pope John Paul II

The future is an infinite succession of presents,
and to live now as we think human beings should live,
in defiance of all that is bad around us,
is itself a marvelous victory.

—Howard Zinn, historian

The only limit to our realization of tomorrow
will be our doubts of today.
Let us move forward with strong and active faith.

—Franklin Delano Roosevelt, Jefferson Day speech, written the night before he died

9

RELATIONSHIPS

Neither a lofty degree of intelligence nor imagination nor both together go to the making of genius. Love, love, love, that is the soul of genius.

Wolfgang Amadeus Mozart

It's all very well to talk about you as an individual and about your life, your character, or your fortunes in isolation. But of course none of those things really exist in isolation, even for those of us who live the most solitary lives. This chapter invites us to ponder the nature of the interactions that collectively create our relationships with other individuals.

Relationships with other people can bring us some of our greatest joys, but they can also be a source of some of our most intense sorrows and frustrations. They can bring out the best or the worst in our characters; most of the virtues we aspire to don't really come into play until we practice them in our relationships. And other people have, in George Eliot's words, "an equivalent centre of self, whence the lights and shadows must always fall with a certain difference." Hence they have an unfortunate tendency to not fit neatly into our own plans. It is what we do when other people mess up our plans that determines whether we live with a greater or lesser degree of love.

In this chapter, I've focused more on the difficult side of relationships than on the times when everything is lovely, chiefly because I believe it's the difficult things that we need to hear more about. There's more for us to do there. But quotations about the positive side of relationships are here too; they can show us what we're striving for, or remind us of the value of the relationships we have.

To know and love one other human being is the
root of all wisdom.

—Evelyn Waugh, *Brideshead*

Life is a drama, not a monologue.

—Edward Bulwer-Lytton, *The Caxtons*

The more you feel anchored in your inner being and can validate
your own opinions, feelings and desires, the more you can give to
others and truly listen to others without fear of losing yourself.

—Helene G. Brenner, *I Know I'm in There Somewhere*

It is easier to live through someone else
than to become complete yourself.

—Betty Friedan, *The Feminine Mystique*

You bring all you ever were and are to any relationship
you have today.

—Fred Rogers

Love is, above all, the gift of oneself.

—Jean Anouilh, *Ardèle*

Always there remain portions of our heart into which
no one is able to enter, invite them as we may.

—Mary Dixon Thayer, *Things to Live By*

Every human creature is constituted
to be that profound secret
and mystery to every other.

—Charles Dickens, *A Tale of Two Cities*

None of us has the power to make someone else love us.
But **we all have the power to give away love**,
to love other people. And if we do so,
we change the kind of person we are,
and we change the kind of world we live in.

—Rabbi Harold Kushner

The respect given to others rebounds to the giver;
to deny the sacred in the Other is to deny it in oneself.

—Dr. Raymond Johnson

Love is the extremely difficult realization that something other than oneself is real.

–Iris Murdoch

To fear love is to fear life, and those who fear life
are already three parts dead.

—Bertrand Russell, *Marriage and Morals*

Life is short and we have never too much time for gladdening the hearts of those who are traveling the dark journey with us. Oh, be swift to love, make haste to be kind!

—Henri-Frédéric Amiel, *The Journal Intime of Henri-Frédéric Amiel,* translated by Mrs. Humphry Ward

Life is short, but there is always time for courtesy.

—Ralph Waldo Emerson, *Letters and Social Aims*

Always be nice to all the people who can't talk back to you. I can't stand a man or woman who bawls out underlings to satisfy an ego.

—Harry S. Truman

Perhaps that is what love is—the momentary or prolonged refusal to
think of another person in terms of power.

—Phyllis Rose

The great question in life is the suffering we cause;
and the utmost ingenuity of metaphysics
cannot justify the man who has pierced
the heart that loved him.

—Benjamin Constant, French novelist, political philosopher, and politician

Mortals are easily tempted to pinch the life out of their neighbour's buzzing
glory, and think that such killing is no murder.

—George Eliot, *Middlemarch*

Some persons, by hating vices too much, come to love men too little.

—Edmund Burke

We must learn to love in the absence of illusions.

—Sheldon B. Kopp, *What Took You So Long?*

Love takes off the mask that we fear
we cannot live with and know
we cannot live without.

—Robert Slater

Wisdom in loving is allowing the
different seasons of love.
It is not always spring.

—Sam Keen, *To a Dancing God: Notes of a Spiritual Traveler*

Love is never wasted; love is never lost. Love lives on and
sees us through sorrow. From the moment love is born, it
is always with us, keeping us aloft in the time of flooding
and strong in the time of trial.

—Ronald Reagan, remarks at the memorial service for members of the Army's 101st Airborne
Division, killed in an airplane crash, Fort Campbell, Kentucky, December 16, 1985

Love is the strongest force the world possesses and yet it is the humblest imaginable.

—Mahatma Gandhi, *All Men Are Brothers*

Even love cannot completely alter the course of life in a moment.

—Arlo Bates, *Puritans*, XI

She did observe, with some dismay, that, far from conquering all, love lazily sidestepped practical problems.

—Jean Stafford

True belonging is born of relationships not only to one another but to a place of shared responsibilities and benefits. We love not so much what we have acquired as what we have made and whom we have made it with.

—Robert Finch, "Scratching," *The Primal Place*

Familiar acts are beautiful through love.

—Percy Bysshe Shelley

Love me, my brothers, for I am infinitely necessary to you
and for your delight I was made. . . . Love me, my brothers,
for I am infinitely superfluous, and your love shall be like His,
born neither of your need nor of my deserving, but a plain bounty.

—C. S. Lewis, *Perelandra*

For nothing among human things
has such power to keep our gaze fixed
ever more intensely upon God,
than friendship for the friends of God.

—Simone Weil

The people I love best, I love for their spiritual quality, for it shows me God somehow, and I hunger for him even when I am least positive of his being underneath us all.

—Ellen Glasgow, *Letters of Ellen Glasgow*

We are over-hasty to speak—as if God did not manifest himself by our silent feeling, and make his love felt through ours.

—George Eliot, *Adam Bede*

The best friends are those who know how to keep the same silences.

—Bishop Fulton J. Sheen

To communicate is natural; to accept what is communicated
is an acquired art.

—Johann Wolfgang von Goethe, *Elective Affinities*

All the problems of the world are caused by
people who do not listen.

—Franco Zeffirelli, quoted in *The Observer*, 1998

It takes a great man to make a good listener.

—Sir Arthur Helps, *Brevia*

The difference between listening and pretending to listen, I discovered, is enormous. One is fluid, the other is rigid. One is alive, the other is stuffed. Eventually, I found a radical way of thinking about listening. **Real listening is a willingness to let the other person change you.**

—Alan Alda, *Never Have Your Dog Stuffed and Other Things I've Learned*

I've always believed that a lot of the troubles in the world would disappear if we were talking to each other instead of about each other.

—Ronald Reagan, remarks at the Ford Motor Company's Claycomo assembly plant, April 11, 1984

It is as easy to recall a stone thrown violently from the hand as a word which has left your tongue.

—Menander

Love and trust, in the space between what's said
and what's heard in our life,
can make all the difference in this world.

—Fred Rogers

Men exist for each other.
Then either improve them, or put up with them.

—Marcus Aurelius, *Meditations*

It is easier to love humanity as a whole than to love one's neighbor.

—Eric Hoffer

If we could read the secret history of our enemies,
we should find in each man's life sorrow
and suffering enough to disarm all hostility.

—Henry Wadsworth Longfellow

You cannot judge any man beyond your knowledge of him,
and how small is your knowledge.

—Kahlil Gibran, *Sand and Foam*

How little any of us know of the real internal state even of those whom we see most frequently.

—Samuel Johnson, quoted in *The Life of Samuel Johnson* by James Boswell

The price of hating other human beings is loving oneself less.

—Eldridge Cleaver, *Soul on Ice*

It is now long ago that I . . . resolved that I would permit no man, no matter what his colour might be, to narrow and degrade my soul by making me hate him.

—Booker T. Washington, *Up from Slavery: An Autobiography*

Hatred toward any human being cannot exist in the same heart as love to God.

—William Ralph Inge, Dean of St. Paul's Cathedral

The worst sin towards our fellow creatures is not to hate them, but to be indifferent to them. That's the essence of inhumanity.

—George Bernard Shaw, *The Devil's Disciple*

Forgiveness is not an occasional act; it is a permanent attitude.

—Martin Luther King, Jr.

Our self-centeredness, our distinctive attachment to the feeling of an independent, self-existent "I," works fundamentally to inhibit our compassion. Indeed, true compassion can be experienced only when this type of self-grasping is eliminated. But this does not mean that we cannot start and make progress now.

—Tenzin Gyatso the Fourteenth Dalai Lama

Forgiveness is the grace by which you enable the other person to get up, and get up with dignity, to begin anew. Not to forgive leads to bitterness and hatred, which gnaw away at the vitals of one's being.

—Desmond Tutu

Those you do not forgive you fear.
And no one reaches love with fear beside him.

—From *A Course in Miracles*, published by the Foundations for Inner Peace

Oftentimes I have hated in self-defense;
but **if I were stronger**
I would not have used such a weapon.

—Kahlil Gibran, *Sand and Foam*

Treat your enemies with courtesy, and you'll see how valuable it really is. It costs little, but pays a nice dividend: Those who honor are honored. Politeness and a sense of honor have this advantage: We bestow them on others without losing a thing.

—Baltazar Gracián

The one thing I learned in loving my grandmother is that you can love someone not for their qualities but for their defects. You can love someone because of their difference with you not because of their similarities with you.

—Guillermo del Toro, director of *Pan's Labyrinth*, in an interview with Terry Gross, *Fresh Air* January 24, 2007

There is nowhere you can go and
only be with people who are like you.
Give it up.

—Bernice Johnson Reagon

To care about people who are fearful, angry, jealous, overpowered by addictions of all kinds, arrogant, proud, miserly, selfish, mean, you name it—to have compassion and to care for these people means not to run from the pain of finding these things in ourselves.

—Pema Chodron

When someone is acting difficult to love,
that usually means they are needing it terribly.

—Margaret Anne Huffman

Never get too close to a man who hates himself.

—Naguib Mahfouz, *Miramar*

If your heart is a volcano how shall you expect flowers to bloom in your hands?

—Kahlil Gibran, *Sand and Foam*

You cannot live with a chip on your shoulder
even if you can manage a smile around your eyes.
For chips make you bend your body to balance them.
And once you bend, you lose your poise, your balance,
and the chip gets into you. The real you. You get hard.

—Marita Bonner

It is a comfortable thought that the smallest and most turbid mud-puddle can contain its own picture of heaven. Let us remember this when we feel inclined to deny all spiritual life to some people, in whom, nevertheless, Our Father may perhaps see the image of His face.

—Nathaniel Hawthorne

**We love those who know the worst of us
and don't turn their faces away.**

—Walker Percy

True friendship, like a diamond,
radiates steadily from its transparent heart.

—Lydia M. Child

Without friends no one would choose to live,
though he had all other goods.

—Aristotle

True friendship is a plant of slow growth,
and must undergo and withstand the shock
of adversity before it is entitled to the appellation.

—George Washington, to Bushrod Washington, January 15, 1783

It is not so much our friends' help that helps us
as the confident knowledge that they will help us.

—Epicurus

He was only a fox like a hundred thousand other foxes.
But I have made him my friend,
and now he is unique in all the world.

—Antoine de Saint Exupéry, *The Little Prince*

Marriage: the only adventure open to the cowardly.

—Voltaire

It is the nature of love to bind itself, and the institution of marriage merely paid the average man the compliment of taking him at his word.

—G. K. Chesterton

Chains do not hold a marriage together.
It is threads, hundreds of tiny threads
which sew people together through the years.

—Simone Signoret, quoted in *Daily Mail*, July 4, 1978

I know one husband and wife who, whatever the official reasons given to the court for the break up of their marriage, were really divorced because the husband believed that nobody ought to read while he was talking and the wife that nobody ought to talk while she was reading.

—Vera Brittain

The great gift of family life is to be intimately acquainted with people you might never even introduce yourself to, had life not done it for you.

—Kendall Hailey, *The Day I Became an Autodidact*

The great advantage of living in a large family is that early lesson of life's essential unfairness.

—Nancy Mitford

We can do without an extended family as human beings about as easily as we can do without vitamins or essential minerals.

—Kurt Vonnegut Jr.

Better to be driven out from among men
than to be disliked of children.

—Richard Henry Dana

No man can possibly know what life means, what the world means, until he has a child and loves it. And then the whole universe changes, and nothing will ever seem exactly as it seemed before.

—Lafcadio Hearn

Raising children is the best thing I've ever done.
Being a mother is what I think has made me the person I am.

—Jacqueline Kennedy Onassis

Bringing up a family should be an adventure, not an anxious discipline in which everybody is constantly graded for performance.

—Milton R. Sapirstein, *Paradoxes of Everyday Life*

If a child has sinned all have sinned.

—Kikuyu proverb (from Kenya)

If we had paid no more attention to plants
than we have to our children,
we would now be living in a jungle of weeds.

—Luther Burbank

As the twig is bent the tree inclines.

—Virgil

There are only two lasting bequests
we can hope to give our children.
One of these is roots; the other, wings.

—Hodding Carter

Every kid starts out as a natural-born scientist, and then we beat it out of them.

—Carl Sagan, *Psychology Today*

We must believe the things we teach our children.

—Woodrow Wilson

The attitude you have as a parent
is what your kids will learn from
more than what you tell them.
They don't remember what you try to teach them.
They remember what you are.

–Jim Henson

There was a time when we expected
nothing of children but obedience,
as opposed to the present,
when we expect everything of them but obedience.

—Anatole Broyard, *Books of the Times*

Trust, and not submission, defines obedience.

—Joan W. Blos, *A Gathering of Days*

It seems to me that we are doing things
we do not want to do for kids
who do not really want to have them done.

—Robert Paul Smith, "Let Your Kids Alone," *Life*, January 27, 1958

In the final analysis it is not what you do for your children
but what you taught them to do for themselves
that will make them successful human beings.

—Ann Landers

Children cannot be made good by making them happy,
but they can be made happy by making them good.

—E. J. Kiefer

The lack of emotional security of our American young people
is due, I believe, to their isolation from the larger family unit.
No two people . . . are enough to provide emotional security
for a child. He needs to feel himself one in a world of kinfolk,
persons of variety in age and temperament,
and yet allied to himself by an indissoluble bond.

—Pearl S. Buck

Hug [your] grandparents and say 'I want to thank you for what
you've done to make me and my life possible.'

—Alex Haley

Children are the living messages we send to a time we will not see.

—John W. Whitehead

Our children are not going to be just "our children"—
they are going to be other people's husbands and wives and
the parents of our grandchildren.

—Mary Steichen Calderone

We worry about what a child will become tomorrow, yet we forget that he is someone today.

—Stacia Tauscher

I just kept saying how this world
was a terrible place to try and bring up a child in.
And Lou Ann kept saying,
For God's sake,
what other world have we got?

—Barbara Kingsolver, *The Bean Trees*

10

THE SELF IN THE WORLD

When a true genius appears in this world you may know him by this sign, that the dunces are all in confederacy against him.

Jonathan Swift

Although our friends, neighbors, and family are the other selves that we have the most concrete contact with, our interactions with the world don't stop there. Each of us is a self in a larger world, a world of people and plants, animals and objects—and of the social, political, economic, and technological networks that both connect and separate them.

The fact that we are selves in a larger world works both ways: the world affects us, and we affect it, whether we are aware of it or not. Obviously, these effects can be both good and bad; common decency demands that we try to minimize the evil we do. We won't eliminate it; try as we might, we will cause suffering and evil around us. But we can at least attempt to reduce it, and ideally increase the good we do as well. The better we understand the multiple complex interrelationships between all the different parts of the world, the more ably we will be able to direct our actions towards the goals we have in mind.

Part of that great chaotic mix of what goes on in the world is, of course, the action of all the other people in it, singly and in groups or masses. This chapter explores some of the tensions in the relationships between individuals and the society around them.

Considering the multitude of forms interactions between the self and the world can take, this chapter can barely scratch the surface of the topic. I have for the most part selected quotes that treat the subject in a general way; many of them could be applicable to a number of different social issues. There's also, of course, some overlap with Chapter 1. There, we considered the connection between ourselves and the larger world from a cosmic or spiritual standpoint. Here, the overall viewpoint is more practical. Ultimately, we can no more divorce the spiritual completely from the practical than we can separate the self from the world; it's all interconnected.

The world is before you, and you need not take it or leave it as it was when you came in.

—James Baldwin

I am life which wills to live
in the midst of other life which wills to live.
I must therefore revere my own life and all other life around me.

—Albert Schweitzer

Man shapes himself through decisions that shape his environment.

—René Dubois

What is not good for the beehive,
cannot be good for the bees.

—Marcus Aurelius, *Meditations*

The throwing out of balance of the resources
of nature throws out of balance also the lives of men.

—Franklin Delano Roosevelt

The highly industrialized Western world has neglected to the utmost degree to leave room for man . . . The individual has become a tool. He hardly has any contact with nature anymore. That is, with himself. He has lost his soul and is not even trying to find it again.

—Indira Gandhi

Technology : the knack of so arranging
the world that we need not experience it.

—Max Frisch, *Homo Faber*

All of us need to keep in touch
with wild, unruly things, even if we do it
in the tamest possible way.

—Maggie Nichols, *Wild, Wild Woman*

In the spring, at the end of the day, you should smell like dirt.

—Margaret Atwood

**To forget how to dig the earth
and to tend the soil
is to forget ourselves.**

—Mohatma Gandhi

All through the long winter, I dream of my garden.
On the first day of spring, I dig my fingers deep into the soft earth.
I can feel its energy, and my spirits soar.

—Helen Hayes

Every word and every being come knocking at your door, bringing you their mystery. If you are open to them, they will flood you with their riches.

—Irénée Guilana Dioh

If you love everything you will perceive the divine mystery in things. Once you perceive it, you will begin to comprehend it better every day. **And you will come to love the whole world with an all-embracing love.**

—Fyodor Dostoevsky

Where is our comfort but in the free, uninvolved, finally mysterious beauty and grace of this world that we did not make, that has no price? Where is our sanity but there? **Where is our pleasure but in working and resting kindly in the presence of this world?**

—Wendell Berry, "Economy and Pleasure," in *What Are People For?*

I believe that one of the great problems
for us as individuals is the depression
and the tension resulting from existence
in a world which is increasingly
less pleasing to the eye.

—Lady Bird Johnson

Day after day, my faith confirms that man's purity
is as much from outside as it is from inside,
and that **we must provide light and clean air
if we want beautiful flowers.**

—Naguib Mahfouz, *Mirrors*

If we don't sit down and shut up once in a while we'll lose our minds even earlier than we had expected. Noise is an imposition on sanity, and we live in very noisy times.

—Joan Báez, *Daybreak*

We each have a moral obligation to conserve and preserve beauty in this world; there is none to waste.

—Robert A. Heinlein, *Friday*

Everybody needs beauty as well as bread,
places to play in and pray in,
where Nature may heal and cheer
and give strength to body and soul alike.

—John Muir, *The Yosemite*

Parts of the earth, once living and productive,
have died at the hand of man.
Others are now dying. If we cause more to die,
Nature will compensate for this in her own way,
inexorably, as already she has begun to do.

—Fairfield Osborn, *Our Plundered Planet*

We do not weave the web of life,
We are merely a strand in it.
Whatever we do to the web,
We do to ourselves.

—Chief Seattle

Eating with the fullest pleasure—pleasure, that is, that does not depend on ignorance—is perhaps the profoundest enactment of our connection with the world. In this pleasure we experience and celebrate our dependence and our gratitude, for we are living from mystery, from creatures we did not make and powers we cannot comprehend.

—Wendell Berry, "The Pleasures of Eating," in *What Are People For?*

Half the world is starving; the other half is on a diet.
We are not privileged because we deserve to be.
Privilege accepted should mean responsibility accepted.

—Madeleine L'Engle

I recognize the right and duty of this generation to develop and use our natural resources, but I do not recognize the right to waste them, or to rob by wasteful use, the generations that come after us.

—Theodore Roosevelt

The conspicuous consumption
of limited resources has yet to be
accepted widely as a spiritual error,
or even bad manners.

—Barbara Kingsolver, *Animal, Vegetable, Miracle*

Consumption used to be the name for a mortal wasting disease. It still is.

—Anna Quindlen, "Don't Mess with Mother," *Newsweek* September 19, 2005

The Economy is, literally, rooted in the Ecosystem. Money doesn't grow on trees, but as trees.

—Mylo Roze, founder of Holistic Affordable Housing and producer ofWME3tv

Money is the root of all evil, and yet it is such a useful root that we cannot get on without it any more than we can without potatoes.

—Louisa May Alcott, *Little Men*

Money is like muck,
not good except it be spread.

—Francis Bacon, *Essays*

Rats and roaches live by competition under the law of supply and demand; it is the privilege of human beings to live under the laws of justice and mercy.

—Wendell Berry, "Economy and Pleasure," in *What Are People For?*

No one can . . . love his neighbor on an empty stomach.

—Woodrow Wilson

The less we have, the more we give.
Seems absurd, but it's the logic of love.

—Mother Teresa

Money-giving is a good criterion of a person's mental health.
Generous people are rarely mentally ill people.

—Karl Menninger

It is physically impossible for a well-educated, intellectual, or brave man to make money the chief object of his thoughts; just as it is for him to make his dinner the principal object of them.

—John Ruskin, *The Crown of Wild Olive*

Those who never think of money need a great deal of it.

—Agatha Christie

The animal needing something knows how much it needs, the man does not.

—Democritus of Abdera

**Nothing is cheap which is superfluous,
for what one does not need, is dear at a penny.**

—Plutarch, *Lives*

The fundamental, vital thing which must be alive in each human consciousness is the religious teaching that we cannot live for ourselves alone and that as long as we are here on this earth we are all of us brothers, regardless of race, creed, or color.

—Eleanor Roosevelt, "What Religion Means to Me," *The Forum* 88, December 1932

There are people and things in this world, and people are
to be loved and things are to be used.
And it is increasingly important
that we love people and use things, for there is so much
in our gadget-minded, consumer-oriented society
that is encouraging us to love things and use people.

—William Sloane Coffin

We must save ourselves from
the products that we are asked
to buy in order, ultimately,
to replace ourselves.

—Wendell Berry, from "Feminism, the Body, and the Machine,"
in *What Are People For?*

We must ensure that color, race and gender become only a God-given gift to each one of us and not an indelible mark or attribute that accords a special status to any.

—Nelson Mandela

It has always been a mystery to me
how men can feel themselves honoured
by the humiliation of their fellow beings.

—Mahatma Gandhi, *All Men Are Brothers*

[W]hile there is a lower class, I am in it; while there is a criminal element, I am of it; while there is a soul in prison, I am not free.

—Eugene V. Debs, upon being sentenced to jail for opposing the First World War

In all people I see myself, none more and not one a barley-corn less,
And the good or bad I say of myself I say of them.

—Walt Whitman, *Song of Myself*

Good and evil we know in the field of this world
grow up together almost inseparably.

—John Milton, *Areopagitica*

**O, mickle is the powerful grace that lies
In plants, herbs, stones, and their true qualities.**
For naught so vile that on the earth doth live
But to the earth some special good doth give;
Nor aught so good but, strain'd from that fair use,
Revolts from true birth, stumbling on abuse.
Virtue itself turns vice being misapplied,
And vice sometime's by action dignified.

—William Shakespeare, *Romeo and Juliet*, II.iii

Politics is not something to avoid, abolish, or destroy. It is a
condition like the atmosphere we breathe. It is something to live
with, to influence if we wish, and to control if we can. We must
master its ways or we shall be mastered by those who do.

—Raymond Moley

To give up the task of reforming society
is to give up one's responsibility as a free man.

—Alan Paton, South African writer, 'The Challenge of Fear,'
Saturday Review, September, 9, 1967

Freedom is a precious thing, and the inalienable
birthright of all who travel this earth.

—Paul Robeson

Man is condemned to be free.

—Jean-Paul Sartre

Freedom is having a pure and dauntless heart;
all else is slavery and lies hidden in darkness.

—Quintus Ennius

Resolve, and thou art free.

—Henry Wadsworth Longfellow

The capacity to get free is nothing;

the capacity to be free, that is the task.

—André Gide

To be free is not merely to cast off one's chains,
but to live in a way that respects and
enhances the lives of others.

—Nelson Mandela, *The Star*, August 22, 1997

Freedom knows no borders . . .
a fiery voice of liberty in one country
can raise the spirits of another far away.

—Kofi Annan, address at the John Fitzgerald Kennedy Library, Boston, 6 June 1997

Everybody wants to do something to help,
but nobody wants to be first.

—Pearl Bailey

Leadership is the art of getting other people to run with your idea as if it were their own.

—Harry S. Truman

Alone we can do so little; together we can do so much.

—Helen Keller

It is better to be part of a great whole than to be the whole of a small part.

—Frederick Douglass, interview, Anacostia, Washington, D. C., January 1889

I have always held firmly to the thought that each one of us can do a little to bring some portion of misery to an end.

—Albert Schweitzer

When you cease to make a contribution, you begin to die.

—Eleanor Roosevelt, in letter to Mr. Home, February 19, 1960

Our lives begin to end the day we become silent about things that matter.

—Martin Luther King, Jr.

God provided me with the strength I needed at the precise time
when conditions were ripe for change.
I am thankful to Him every day that
He gave me the strength not to move.

—Rosa Parks on the Montgomery bus boycott

How lovely to think that no one need wait a moment: we can
start now, start slowly changing the world! How lovely that
everyone, great and small, can make a contribution toward
introducing justice straight away.

—Anne Frank

Opportunities of doing good, though abundant, and obvious enough, are not exactly fitted to our hands; we must be alert in preparing ourselves for them. Benevolence requires method and activity in its exercise.

—Sir Arthur Helps, *Essays Written in the Intervals of Business*

Those who want to do good are not selfish.
They are not in a hurry.
They know that to impregnate people with good
requires a long time. But evil has wings.
To build a house takes time.
Its destruction takes none.

—Mahatma Ghandi, *Hind Swaraj*

The devil loves nothing better than the intolerance of reformers, and dreads nothing so much as their charity and patience.

—James Russell Lowell

The serene, silent beauty of a holy life
is the most powerful influence in the world,
next to the might of God.

—Blaise Pascal

You can preach a better sermon with your life than with your lips.

—Oliver Goldsmith

Ah! It is so easy to convert others.
It is so difficult to convert oneself.

—Oscar Wilde, *The Critic as Artist*

Each time anyone comes in contact with us,
they must become different and better people
because of having met us. We must radiate God's love.

—Mother Teresa

The divine bounty wishes to be visible today . . . present through our love.

—Pope John Paul II

Make peace with someone you think you can't make peace with.
Notice what resistance arises even at the thought, how you build
your case against your enemy, how you marshal your allies and
ready your weapons. Note what it takes to give them up, what you
must sacrifice and what you gain.

—Starhawk

We have learned as common knowledge
that much of the insensibility and hardness of the world
is due to the lack of imagination which prevents
a realization of the experiences of other people.

—Jane Addams, Introduction, *Democracy and Social Ethics*

If the misery of others leaves you indifferent
and with no feeling of sorrow,
then you cannot be called a human being.

—Jimmy Carter, *Keeping Faith*

A different world cannot be built by indifferent people.

—Horace Mann, philosopher

That which is everybody's business is nobody's business.

—Izaak Walton

In every community there is work to be done. In every nation, there are wounds to heal. In every heart, there is the power to do it.

—Marianne Williamson

You can't live a perfect day without doing something for someone who will never be able to repay you.

—John Wooden

I have always believed that you help people one at a time. That's how lives are changed.

—Oprah Winfrey

Each of us must work for his own improvement,
and at the same time share a general responsibility
for all humanity, our particular duty being
to aid those to whom we think
we can be most useful.

—Marie Curie

No man is an island, entire of itself; every man is a piece of the continent, a part of the main. If a clod be washed away by the sea, Europe is the less, as well as if a promontory were, as well as if a manor of thy friend's or of thine were.

—John Donne, *Meditation 17*

Any man's death diminishes me, because I am involved in mankind; and therefore never send to know for whom the bell tolls; it tolls for thee.

—John Donne, *Meditation 17*

All the miseries of mankind come from one thing, not knowing how to remain alone.

—Blaise Pascal, *Pensées*

We need other human beings in order to be human.
The solitary, isolated human being is really a contradiction in terms.

—Desmond Tutu

Every man who is truly a man must learn to be alone
in the midst of all others, and if need be against all others.

—Romain Rolland

If all mankind minus one, were of one opinion, and only one person
were of the contrary opinion, mankind would be no more justified
in silencing that one person, than he, if he had the power, would be
justified in silencing mankind.

—John Stuart Mill

Every time a person is deprived of the right to think
I feel a child of mine has been murdered.

—José Martí

It is because we have at the present moment everybody claiming the right
of conscience without going through any discipline whatsoever that there
is so much untruth being delivered to a bewildered world.

—Mahatma Gandhi, *All Men Are Brothers*

In the last analysis our only freedom
is the freedom to discipline ourselves.

—Bernard Baruch

Let us not be bubbled then out of our reverence
and obedience to government on one hand;
nor out of our right to think and act for ourselves
in our own department on the other.

—John Adams, "On Self-Delusion," *Boston Gazette*, August 29, 1763

Some people were sitting in a ship, when one of them took a drill and began to bore a hole under his seat. The other passengers protested to him, 'What are you doing?' He answered, 'What has this to do with you? Am I not boring the hole under my own seat?' They retorted, 'But the water will come in and drown us all.'

—Leviticus Rabbah 4:6

When we try to pick out anything by itself,
we find it hitched to everything else in the universe.

—John Muir

There is no sort of wrong deed of which a man can bear
the punishment alone: you can't isolate yourself,
and say that the evil which is in you shall not spread.
**Men's lives are as thoroughly blended with each other
as the air they breathe**: evil spreads as necessarily as disease.

—George Eliot, *Adam Bede*

Insecure people tend to be intolerant,
and their intolerance unleashes forces
that threaten the security of others.

—Daw Aung San Suu Kyi, recipient of the 1991 Nobel Peace Prize, from a speech delivered
(via videotape) to the Non-Governmental Organization Forum on Women in Huairou,
China, August. 31, 1995

There is no security on this earth;
there is only opportunity.

—Douglas MacArthur

Education is the torch that destroys the fear in the heart of man.

—James Malof

Hatred and bitterness can never cure the disease of fear; only love can do that. Hatred paralyzes life; love releases it. Hatred confuses life; love harmonizes it. Hatred darkens life; love illumines it.

—Martin Luther King, Jr.

The conclusion is always the same:
**love is the most powerful and still
the most unknown energy of the world.**

—Pierre Teilhard de Chardin

In God's wildness lies the hope of the world—the great fresh unblighted,
unredeemed wilderness.

—John Muir, note from Alaska, 1890

We can't cure the world of sorrows
but we can choose to live in joy.

—Joseph Campbell

The strongest and sweetest songs yet remain to be sung.

—Walt Whitman, *A Backward Glance O'er Travel'd Roads*

INDEX

A Course in Miracles, 357
Abbey, Edward, 170, 301
Abbott, Shirley, 50
Ackerman, Diane, 302
Adamic, Louis, 13
Adams, Henry, 63
Adams, John, 77, 279, 415
Addams, Jane, 308, 408
Addison, Joseph, 69, 174, 219
Aesop, 139
Agar, Herbert Sebastian, 162
Alcott, A. Bronson, 171
Alcott, Louisa May, 391
Alda, Alan, 285, 351
Alexander, Lloyd,
Allen, George, 73, 212
Amiel, Henri Frederic, 152, 316, 340
Anaxagoras, 4
Angelou, Maya, 70, 241, 242, 247, 260
Annan, Kofi, 401
Anouilh, Jean, 337
Anthony, Robert, 145
Aquinas, Thomas, 25, 266
Aristotle, 119, 192, 363
Arnold, Matthew, 18
Astor, Lady Nancy, 221
Atwood, Margaret, 382
Auden, W. H., 204
Aurelius, Marcus, 59, 352, 381
Bacall, Lauren, 201
Bach, Richard, 32
Bacon, Francis, 114, 391
Báez, Joan, 386
Baha'u'llah, 188
Bailey, Pearl, 72, 136, 401

Baldwin, James, 197, 230, 380
Balzac, Honoré de, 120
Banks, Iain M., 323
Barclay, William, 286
Barrie, Sir J. M., 130, 175
Barry, Dave, 184
Barrymore, Ethel, 310
Barthelme, Don, 307
Barton, Bruce, 271
Baruch, Bernard, 415
Basho, Matsuo, 322
Bates, Arlo, 346
Baum, L. Frank, 94
Beattie, Paul, 177
Becker, Mary Lamberton, 312
Beckett, Samuel, 257
Beecher, Henry Ward, 37, 102, 264,
Bell, Eric T., 132
Bellin, Gita, 106
Bellow, Saul, 96, 327
Benchley, Robert, 119
Benson, A. C., 146
Bernard, Claude, 149
Berry, John, 223
Berry, Wendell, 38, 118, 385, 388, 391, 395
Bhagavad Gita, 37,
Bible, The: Leviticus Rabbah, 416; Psalms, 31
Bierce, Ambrose, 16
Blake, William, 23, 32, 84, 135, 210, 214, 217, 223
Blanchard, Dr. Kenneth, 98
Blanton, Smiley, 318
Blos, Joan W., 371
Blum, Léon, 238
Blum, Ralph H., 191

Bombeck, Erma, 209
Bonhoeffer, Rev. Dietrich, 331
Bosco, Don, 306
Boswell, James, 148, 354
Bourget, Paul, 165
Brandeis, Louis D., 213
Brenner, Helene G., 336
Brittain, Vera, 365
Browder, Charles, 151
Brown, Jr., H. Jackson, 297
Brown, William Wells, 327
Browning, Robert, 160
Broyard, Anatole, 371
Brunner, Emil, 17
Bruyn, Joshua, 153
Bryan, William Jennings, 233
Buber, Martin, 27
Buck, Pearl S., 306, 373
Buffett, Warren, 323
Bulwer-Lytton, Edward, 130, 336
Burbank, Luther, 369
Burke, Edmund, 97, 186, 342
Buscaglia, Leo, 107
Bushman, Kung, 314
Butler, Samuel, 10, 11, 16, 57, 93, 156
Byrom, Thomas, 228
Calderone, Mary Steichen, 374
Campbell, Joseph, 231, 420,
Camus, Albert, 21, 331
Capote, Truman, 207
Carlyle, Thomas, 120, 122, 176
Carter, Hodding, 369
Carter, Jimmy, 409
Carver, George Washington, 50
Castle, Barbara, 146
Cather, Willa, 226

Chandogya Upanishad, 5
Chapin, E. H., 96
Chávez, César, 182, 260, 287
Cheever, Susan, 303
Chesterton, G. K., 27, 93, 364
Chief Joseph, 152
Chief Seattle, 388
Child, Julia, 220
Child, Lydia M., 362
Chodron, Pema, 360
Chopin, Frédéric, 193
Chopra, Deepak, 87, 286, 307
Chraïbi, Driss, 41
Christian, John, 9
Christie, Agatha, 13, 393
Churchill, Winston, 96, 110, 114, 128, 150,
    182, 250, 267, 330
Cicero, 97
Cleaver, Eldridge, 354
Coffin, William Sloane, 12, 54, 135, 163, 395
Cole, Johnnetta B., 172, 208, 227
Coleridge, Samuel Taylor, 74, 305
Colette, 189
Collingwood, R. G., 118
Collins, Churton, 169
Collins, Marva N., 24
Colton, Charles Caleb, 65, 300
Connolly, Cyril, 79
Conrad, Joseph, 185
Constant, Benjamin, 341
Constantine, David, 71
Cooke, Alistair, 125
Coolidge, Calvin, 20
Coover, Robert, 71
Cousins, Norman, 76
Covey, Stephen, 262

Coward, Noël, 19, 98, 116, 194, 312
Creech, Sharon, 212
Croquette, Sonia, 209
Crosby, Ernest, 138
Cumberland, Bishop Richard, 125
cummings, e. e., 49
Curie, Marie, 33, 197, 411
Dahlberg, Edward, 208
Dana, Richard Henry, 367
Darrow, Clarence, 162
Darwin, Charles, 40
Davis, Rebecca Harding, 190
Debs, Eugene V., 396
del Toro, Guillermo, 157, 359
Democritus of Abdera, 393
Dewey, John, 109
Dickens, Charles, 338
Dickinson, Emily, 7
Dinesen, Isak, 269, 319
Dioh, Irénée Guilana, 384
Disney, Walt, 309
Donne, John, 411, 412
Dostoevsky, Fyodor, 384
Douglass, Frederick, 240, 402
Dreiser, Theodore, 344
Dubois, René, 380
Dylan, Bob, 159, 254, 277,
Earhart, Amelia, 199
Eastman, Max, 256
Edison, Thomas A., 116, 164, 253, 276
Edwards, Tryon, 63
Ehrmann, Max, 81
Einstein, Albert, 29, 144, 229, 261, 297, 313
Eisenhower, Dwight D., 250
Eisler, Riane, 166
Eliot, Charles W., 226

Eliot, George, 76, 79, 163, 237, 255, 315, 330
Ellison, Ralph, 18
Emerson, Ralph Waldo, vii, 5, 31, 41, 56, 58, 92, 228, 278, 327, 340
Ennius, Quintus, 400
Epicurus, 363
Epstein, Joseph, 235
Erasmus, Desiderius, 69
Escalante, Jaime, 51
Etienne, Jean-Louis, 252
Euripides, 259
Falter-Barns, Suzanne, 208
Feather, William, 254
Ferber, Edna, 132
Feynman, Richard P., 263
Fielding, Henry, 100
Finch, Robert, 347
Firestone, Harvey, 146, 249
Fitzgerald, Zelda, 11
Flaubert, Gustave, 329
Fonteyn, Margot, 83
Foundations for Inner Peace, 357
France, Anatole, 293
Frank, Anne, 404
Franklin, Benjamin, 106, 217, 292, 304
Frazier, Charles, 126
Friedan, Betty, 337
Frisch, Max, 382
Fromm, Erich, 46
Frost, Robert, 124, 224
Fuller, R. Buckminster, 184, 329
Fuller, Thomas, 237
Galen, 117
Galileo, 149
Galsworthy, John, 140, 193
Gandhi, Indira, 177, 381

Gandhi, Mahatma, 108, 192, 280, 346, 396, 405, 414
Gardner, John W., 123
Gautama, Siddhartha, 75, 157, 228
Gehrig, Lou, 189
George, Chief Dan, 75
Getty, J. Paul, 248
Gibran, Kahlil, 83, 210, 233, 353, 358, 361
Gide, André, 55, 400
Gilbert, William Schwenck, 187
Gilman, Charlotte Perkins, 9
Glasgow, Ellen, 349
Goethe, Johann Wolfgang von, ix, 9, 65, 68, 181, 350
Goldman, Francisco, 232
Goldsmith, Oliver, 406
Goodman, Ellen, 282
Gracián, Baltazar, 358
Graham, Sheila, 211
Greene, Brian, 30
Griffiths, Bede, 36
Gyatso, Tenzin, 47, 77, 225, 356
Hafen, Bruce C., 288
Hafiz, 80
Hailey, Kendall, 366
Haldane, J. B. S., 67
Haley, Alex, 191, 373
Hardy, Thomas, 19, 147, 214, 263
Harris, Ann, 48
Harris, Sydney J., 135, 145, 294, 310, 313
Harris, W. Edward, 47, 50, 240
Havel, Vaclev, 181
Hawking, Stephen, 4
Hawthorne, Nathaniel, 362
Hayes, Helen, 383
Hearn, Lafcadio, 367

Hedge, Fredrick Henry, 320
Heinlein, Robert A., 220, 387
Helps, Sir Arthur, 104, 350, 405
Hemingway, Ernest, 115
Henry, Patrick, 142
Henson, Jim, 8, 370
Hepburn, Audrey, 35, 122, 216
Heraclitus, 321
Heschel, Abraham Joshua, 7, 104,
Hillman, James, 306
Hitler, Adolf, 278
Hodnett, Edward, 264
Hoffer, Eric, 353
Holmes, Oliver Wendell, 160, 278
Hood, Thomas, 254
hooks, bell, 317
Howard, Sidney, 213
Hubbard, Frank McKinney, 222
Huffman, Margaret Anne, 360
Hugo, Victor, 2, 10, 151
Hui-k'ung, 231, 265
Hurst, Fannie, 184
Hurston, Zora Neale, 154, 183,
Huxley, Aldous, 158, 189
Inge, William Ralph, 22, 37, 178, 355
Ingersoll, R. G., 200
Irving, Washington, 174, 271
Jackson, Andrew, 52
Jackson, Holbrook, 90
James, William, 17, 147, 167
Jeffers, Robinson, 38
Jefferson, Thomas, 52, 134, 218, 297
Jensen, John, 301
John of the Cross, 28
Johnson, Lady Bird, 259, 385
Johnson, Raymond, 339

Johnson, Samuel, 20, 101, 148, 354
Jong, Erica, 273
Jordan, David Starr, 110
Jordan, Sara, 173
Jung, Carl, 65, 154
Juster, Norton, 239
Kafka, Franz, 313
Kane, Cheikh Hamidou, 64
Keen, Sam, 39, 74, 214, 236, 345
Keller, Helen, 201, 210, 297, 402
Kenji, Miyazawa, 195
Kepler, Johannes, 121
Kiefer, E. J., 372
Kierkegaard, Sören, 68, 318
Killens, John Oliver, 252
King, Jr., Martin Luther, 112, 124, 180, 241, 355, 403, 418
Kingsolver, Barbara, 276, 375, 390
Kissinger, Henry A., 261
Koestenbaum, Peter, 219
Kohn, Hans, 49
Kopp, Sheldon B., 73, 85, 342
Koran, The, 26
Kotter, John, 227
Krimsky, Joseph, 173
Kushner, Rabbi Harold, 190, 338
L'Engle, Madeleine, 311, 389
Laing, R. D., 54
Landers, Ann, 372
Law, William, 238
Lawrence, D. H., 213
Le Gallienne, Richard, 33
Lec, Stanislaw J., 257
Lee, Robert E., 107
LeGuin, Ursula K., 70, 151
Leopold, Aldo, 141, 263

Lessing, Gotthold Ephraim, 319
Lewis, C. S., 6, 131, 205, 239, 348
Lincoln, Abraham, 103, 115, 123, 148, 152, 321
Lindbergh, Anne Morrow, 198, 200, 236, 268
Lindquist, Stanley, 194
Littlebear, Naomi, 193
Locke, John, 66, 134
Lombardi, Vince, 251
Longfellow, Henry Wadsworth, 353, 400
López, Barry, 71, 236
Lorde, Audre, 85
Lowell, James Russell, 406
Luther, Martin, 181
MacArthur, Douglas, 418
MacDonald, George, 74, 82, 215, 231, 283, 299, 316
MacDonald, Peter, 206
MacLaine, Shirley, 61
Madson, Patricia Ryan, 170
Mahfouz, Naguib, 17, 39, 161, 360, 386
Malamud, Bernard, 10
Malik, Charles, 60
Malof, James, 418,
Mandela, Nelson, 111, 199, 284, 396, 401
Mann, Horace, 409
Mann, Thomas, vii, 292
Marden, Orison Swett, 273
Marston, Ralph, 132
Martí, José, 13, 288, 414
Martialis, Marcus Valerius, 316
Mascaro, J., 37
Maugham, W. Somerset, 183, 216
Maxwell, John C., 234
May, Rollo, 28, 29, 85, 156
Mayer, Maria Goeppert, 249

Mayo, William J., 143
Mays, Dr. Benjamin E., 120
Mazrui, Ali A., 234
McKay, David O., 62
McKeithen, Jan, 239
McLaughlin, Mignon, 200
McLuhan, Marshall, 262, 320
Mead, Margaret, 131, 324
Meir, Golda, 194
Menander, 352
Mencius, 20, 185
Menninger, Karl, 392
Mevlevi Dervishes, 34
Mill, John Stuart, 47, 142, 222, 228, 413
Miller, Henry, 137, 272
Mills, C. Wright, 138
Milne, A. A., 129
Milton, John, 34, 397
Mitford, Nancy, 366
Mitropolous, Dimitri, 246
Moley, Raymond, 398
Momaday, N. Scott, 72
Montaigne, Michel de, 229
Montefiore, Claude G., 222
Moore, George, 44, 232
Morris, William, 117
Morrison, Toni, 196
Morrow, Dwight, 116
Mother Teresa, 80, 258, 281, 297, 344, 392, 407
Mozart, Wolfgang Amadeus, 334
Muir, John, 69, 387, 416, 419
Murdoch, Iris, 339
Murray, Pauli, 180
Nachman of Bratslav, 24, 137, 176, 188
Ndaw, Alassane, 28

Nearing, Helen, 36
Needham, Richard J., 101
Neeley, Delma, 242
Nemerov, Howard, 328
Newman, Cardinal J., 303
Nhat Hahn, Thich, 35, 175
Nichols, Maggie, 382
Niebuhr, Reinhold, 158
Nietzsche, Friedrich, 15, 21, 99, 149, 168, 297
O'Connor, Sandra Day, 426, 318,
Okri, Ben, 232
Oliphant, Sir Mark, 320
Onassis, Jacqueline Kennedy, 186, 195, 368
Orben, Robert, 220
Orten, William A., 133
Osborn, Fairfield, 387
Paine, Thomas, 32, 108, 113, 161, 299
Parks, Rosa, 51, 115, 198, 404
Partnow, Susan, 51
Parton, Dolly, 8
Pascal, Blaise, 406, 412
Pasteur, Louis, 159, 248, 297, 326
Patanjali, 274
Paterson, Katherine, 169
Paton, Alan, 399
Paul, Jean, 101
Pauling, Linus, 150
Peale, Norman Vincent, 53, 170, 186
Peck, M. Scott, 56, 73, 136, 224
Percy, Walker, 362
Perkins, Carl, 266
Peters, Roger, 275
Phaedrus, 66
Phelps, William Lyon, 62
Picasso, Pablo, 160
Pilate, Pontius, 129

Plath, Sylvia, 270
Plato, 67, 94, 137, 270
Plutarch, 394
Polanyi, Michael, 290
Pope John Paul II, 162, 331, 407
Pope Paul VI, 283
Pope, Alexander, 52
Powell, Colin, 247, 284
Pratchett, Terry, 158
Price, Doris, 206
Princess Diana, 112
Proust, Marcel, 238
Pythagoras, 8
Quincy, Jr., Josiah, 155
Quindlen, Anna, 11, 79, 122, 155, 390
Rand, Ayn, 219, 277
Reagan, Ronald, 345, 351
Reagon, Bernice Johnson, 359
Rilke, Rainer Maria, 230
Ristad, Eloise, 256
Robeson, Paul, 399
Rochefoucauld, François de La, 211
Rockefeller, John D., 105, 221
Rogers, Fred, 265, 294, 337, 352
Rogers, Will, 95, 134
Rolland, Romain, 413
Roosevelt, Eleanor, 22, 201, 225, 261, 394, 403
Roosevelt, Franklin Delano, 78, 103, 117, 251, 267, 332, 381
Roosevelt, Theodore, 103, 110, 155, 179, 197, 389
Rose, Phyllis, 341
Rossner, Judith, 322
Rosten, Leo, 12
Rousseau, Jean-Jacques, 108

Roze, Mylo, 390
Ruskin, John, 24, 80, 99, 106, 118, 140, 257, 279, 393
Russell, Bertrand, 104, 148, 218, 339
Ruth, Babe, 113
Sagan, Carl, 6, 30, 144, 164, 166, 317, 325, 370
Saint-Exupéry, Antoine de, 105, 138, 343, 364
Sandburg, Carl, 178, 298
Santana, Carlos, 196
Santayana, George, 15, 81, 216, 324, 325
Sapirstein, Milton R., 368
Sarton, May, 284
Sartre, Jean-Paul, 164, 187, 399
Savage, Minot Judson, 33
Sayers, Dorothy L., 121
Schreiner, Olive, 14, 242
Schweitzer, Albert, 246, 266, 380, 403
Scott, Sir Walter, 62. 225, 253
Seneca, 303, 304
Senge, Peter, 113
Shakespeare, William, 301
Shaw, George Bernard, 40, 130, 133, 224, 287, 355
Sheen, Bishop Fulton J., 349
Shelley, Percy Bysshe, 347
Shore, Dinah, 343
Signoret, Simone, 365
Sills, Judith, 78
Singh, Kirpal, 105
Sitting Bull, 55
Skinner, B. F., 64
Slater, Robert, 342
Sloan, Jr., Alfred P., 277
Slovo, Gillian, 285

Smith, Logan Pearsall, 213
Smith, Robert Paul, 371
Smith, Sir Sydney, 305
Sockman, Ralph W., 316
Socrates, 12, 46, 94, 119
Somé, Sobonfu, 23
Sontag, Susan, 139
St. Augustine, 81
St. Benedict, 121
St. Francis de Sales, 78
Stafford, Jean, 346
Stanislas I, 97
Starhawk, 408
Stein, Gertrude, 107
Steinem, Gloria, 61, 196, 237
Sterling, J., 207
Sterne, Laurence, 145
Stevenson, Jr., Adlai E., 107
Stevenson, Robert Louis, 248, 258, 281
Stockdale, James Bond, 95
Stoppard, Tom, 15, 307
Streep, Meryl, 84
Suu Kyi, Daw Aung San, 417
Swift, Jonathan, 139, 379
Tagore, Rabindranath, 133
Tauscher, Stacia, 375
Taylor, Jeremy, 111
Teilhard de Chardin, Pierre, 6, 419
Temple, Sir William, 60, 102
Terence, ix, 217
Thayer, Mary Dixon, 338
Thomas, Marlo, 182
Thoreau, Henry David, 12, 23, 31, 171, 206, 295, 300, 317
Thurber, James, 150, 229, 343
Tolkien, J. R. R., 282

Trollope, Anthony, 323
Truman, Harry S., 124, 233, 296, 340, 402
Tutu, Desmond, 357, 412
Twain, Mark, 58, 59, 100, 147, 179, 187, 199, 280
Ullman, Samuel, 311
Upanishads, The, 25
Updike, John, 57
Valéry, Paul, 234
Van Buren, Abigail, 59
Van Gogh, Vincent, 29, 174
Vélez-Mitchell, Anita, 302
Vienne, Veronique, 272
Virgil, 369
Voltaire, 221, 364
von Rad, Gerhard, 156
Vonnegut, Jr., Kurt, 49, 325, 367
Wagner, Richard, 25
Walker, Alice, 14, 48
Walpole, Horace, 76
Walton, Izaak, 409
Ware, Eugene F., 109
Warren, Rick, 235
Washington, Booker T., 92, 241, 354
Washington, George, 53, 92, 363
Waugh, Evelyn, 44, 336
Wayne, John, 296
Weaver, Earl, 63
Weil, Simone, 159, 275, 348
Wells, H. G., 326
Wharton, Edith, 223
White, Perry A., 153, 283
White, William Hale, 163
Whitehead, Alfred North, 141
Whitehead, John W., 374
Whitman, Walt, 38, 161, 397, 420

Wilde, Oscar, 7, 26, 72, 195, 215, 269, 344,
    407
Wilder, Laura Ingalls, 61, 183, 226, 240, 293
Wilder, Thornton, 154
Williamson, Marianne, 86, 410
Wilson, Major General Louis, 244
Wilson, Woodrow, 370, 392
Winfrey, Oprah, 55, 84, 410
Winters, Jonathan, 114
Wirthlin, Joseph B., 86
Wooden, John, 410
Woolf, Virginia, 57
Wright, Frank Lloyd, 315
Yen-t'ou, 56
Yeshe, Lama Thubten, 27
Yogananda, Paramahansa, 172
Young, Edward, 298
Yunus, Muhammad, 140
Yutang, Lin, 125, 309
Zebrowski, George, 328
Zeffirelli, Franco, 350
Zinn, Howard, 332